Presented To:

_____

From:

_____

Date:

_____

GLIMPSES OF AN INVISIBLE GOD

for Teens

Quiet Reflections to
Refresh and Restore Your Soul

06 05 04 03   10 9 8 7 6 5 4 3 2 1

Glimpses of an Invisible God for Teens
ISBN 1-56292-879-1
Copyright © 2003 by Honor Books,
An Imprint of Cook Communications Ministries
P.O. Box 55388
Tulsa, Oklahoma 74155

Manuscript written by Vicki Kuyper and Stephen Parolini and compiled by Angie Kiesling.

Introduction

More than ever before, people are searching—longing for a deeper relationship with God. Most have no problem recognizing His distinguished hand in the bright hues of the rainbow, the magnificent grandeur of the night sky, the breathtaking vistas of the Grand Canyon. But many of these seekers are hoping for more. *Is He present in the routine moments of my everyday life?* they wonder.

If you have been asking that question, *Glimpses of an Invisible God* is just for you. As you move through its pages, you will enjoy the little stories about people just like you; people who discover that God is really there for them. We have supplied scriptures for each story to guide your reading. Also, you will have an opportunity to learn what can happen when God enters into both the great and small details of your life.

We know you will be blessed as you discover the depth of God's love for you and His commitment to walk with you moment by moment.

The LORD will fight for you;
you need only to be still.

EXODUS 14:14

━

We do live in the world, but we do not
fight in the same way the world fights.

2 CORINTHIANS 10:3 NCV

━

From whence come wars and fightings
among you? come they not hence, even
of your lusts that war in your members?

JAMES 4:1 KJV

━

Glimpses of an Invisible God

"Spending time with God isn't as easy as it sounds," Tammie told her mother. "It's hard to carry on a conversation with Someone you can't see."

"But you can see Him," her mother replied, "if you are looking through the eyes of faith. We can catch glimpses of God every day as we look around us at the things He has created. Most clearly, we can see Him as we look at each other, for we alone of all His creation have been made in His own image.

"Of course God is perfect," she continued, "and human beings clearly aren't. But, at least we know that He created us to be very much like Himself. In that way, we can see Him with our hearts."

Tammie squeezed her mother's hand. "Thanks, Mom," she said. "I think I just saw a glimpse of God in you!"

Look around. You're bound to see God's image in those around you.

MAN IS HEAVEN'S MASTERPIECE.

I will cause showers to come down in their season; there shall be showers of blessing.

EZEKIEL 34:26 NKJV

"I satisfy the weary ones and refresh everyone who languishes."

JEREMIAH 31:25 NASB

Refresh my heart in Christ.

PHILEMON 1:20 RSV

Perfect Moments

There are a few moments in life when everything seems just perfect—when the list for the school play is posted, and your name is across from the lead role. Then there's that time when you realize your lab partner thinks you're oh so much more beautiful than the crystalline formations at the bottom of the test tube.

How about the split-second realization that the most wonderful person in the world is now officially your girlfriend or boyfriend? Or those "may I sit with you?" moments in the cafeteria that come at just the right time to brighten an otherwise overcast day?

But the best moments always seem to have something to do with love. The love of a friend, a parent, or God's love. True love is much greater than we are. It's a taste of the eternal. And those perfect moments are a glimpse of the paradise we were created for.

WHERE LOVE REIGNS, THE VERY JOY OF HEAVEN ITSELF IS FELT.

I have called you by your name; You are Mine.

ISAIAH 43:1 NKJV

Let all those rejoice who put their trust
in You; Let them ever shout for joy,
because You defend them; Let those also
who love Your name be joyful in You.

PSALM 5:11 NKJV

He calls his own sheep by
name and leads them out.

JOHN 10:3

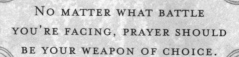

NO MATTER WHAT BATTLE
YOU'RE FACING, PRAYER SHOULD
BE YOUR WEAPON OF CHOICE.

The Battlefield of Life

Lauren heard the school gossip. She knew Sarah had lied, and blaming Lauren provided her with a way out. At first, Lauren asked Sarah to set things straight, but Sarah exploded with angry words of denial.

Lauren wanted to defend herself. But after she took a few minutes to talk to God, she felt Him whisper, "Wait." Lauren still struggled. She bit her tongue whenever Sarah's name came up. But she honored what God had asked her to do.

Months went by. Sarah never changed her story, but something changed in Lauren's heart. Whenever Sarah came to mind or she bumped into her in the hallways, Lauren took a few moments to pray for Sarah. She committed the whole situation to God. She couldn't see what was behind Sarah's lies, but she knew God could. Lauren chose to forgive and move forward.

Are there relationships you need to leave in God's hands today?

Man looks at the outward appearance,
but the LORD looks at the heart.

1 SAMUEL 16:7 NKJV

Everyone who is called by My name,
Whom I have created for My glory;
I have formed him, yes, I have made him.

ISAIAH 43:7 NKJV

I will praise thee; for I am fearfully
and wonderfully made.

PSALM 139:14 KJV

Here's Looking at You

Jeremy dropped his new gym bag on the ottoman and flopped down in front of the television, exhausted. The worn cushions of the couch welcomed him, giving way as needed to accommodate his large frame. He clicked on the television.

"And in only thirty days, you can have a body like this too." Perfectly toned bodies effortlessly demonstrated an "Ab Relocater 3000" device. Jeremy stared across the room into the mirror, sighed, and pushed the off button.

He'd been fat as long as he could remember. Just then the phone rang. It was his friend from youth group, Lynn. "Jeremy—I just wanted to tell you how much I appreciate what you did. You have such a good heart. God must smile when He looks at you."

"God must smile . . ." the words echoed loudly. A smile—from God? Wow! Jeremy took a moment to thank God for helping him see himself in a whole new way—God's way.

Have you ever seen yourself as God sees you?

DON'T ASK THE MIRROR, "HOW DO I LOOK?" ASK GOD.

Clearly, you are a God who
works behind the scenes.

ISAIAH 45:15 THE MESSAGE

The mind of man plans his way,
But the LORD directs his steps.

PROVERBS 16:9 NASB

We know that all things work together for
good to those who love God, to those who
are the called according to His purpose.

ROMANS 8:28 NKJV

Surprise

"God, I hate this school. It's so big that I just feel lost in the crowd. I can't do this much longer! I feel so alone and discouraged," Kristen prayed. "Oh, and, uh, thank You for this food."

Kristen opened her eyes and began to eat just as she had for the past two weeks—alone. A tap on the shoulder startled her. "Kristen! I didn't know you went to school here!"

"Pam?" Kristen looked into the eyes of her new friend from the YMCA. "I can't believe it's you! I just transferred here a couple of weeks ago." Kristen continued shyly, "I guess I'm still a newcomer."

"Not for long," Pam replied with a smile. "Let me introduce you to the gang."

Consider things like unexpected phone calls and chance meetings as surprise glimpses of God's plans for your life. They are not merely coincidences, but special glimpses of God's best for you.

A COINCIDENCE
IS A SMALL
MIRACLE WHERE
GOD PREFERS
TO REMAIN
ANONYMOUS.

What I am commanding you today is not too
difficult for you or beyond your reach.

DEUTERONOMY 30:11

You therefore must endure hardship
as a good soldier of Jesus Christ.

2 TIMOTHY 2:3 NKJV

We can rejoice, too, when we run into
problems and trials, for we know that they are
good for us—they help us learn to endure.

ROMANS 5:3 NLT

FAITH IS TRUST THAT'S BEEN
PUT TO THE TEST.

In God We Trust

Gretchen ran her life like a fine-tuned machine. She could be reached day or night by phone, e-mail, or cell. Her diet was nutritionally balanced. Her social calendar remained full. With the help of her fitness trainer, circle of friends, and fashion websites, she felt she had her life well under control. That is, until the accident.

Gretchen's life changed in a moment. In her hospital bed, she remembered her mother's words: "What you put your trust in makes all the difference in whether you roll with the punches or buckle under the pressure."

Gretchen knew her trust was in the wrong things. Bowing her head, she spent the next few moments asking God to walk with her through the long, painful months of recovery. Immediately, she felt His loving presence fill the room.

Are you placing your trust in the right things or the wrong things?

My soul is downcast within me;
therefore I will remember you.

PSALM 42:6

He will yet fill your mouth with laughter,
and your lips with shouts of joy.

JOB 8:21 NRSV

Peace I leave with you; My peace I give
to you; not as the world gives, do I
give to you. Let not your heart be
troubled, nor let it be fearful.

JOHN 14:27 NASB

Forever Blessed

Depression had been Desiree's companion for as far back as she could remember. Even when nothing was really wrong, she still felt something just wasn't right. Since middle school she had taken anti-depressants and spent time with a therapist. It made her feel like a freak—surely none of the other kids in high school had a shrink!

After a period of time, Desiree's small circle of friends noticed her newfound joy. When they asked what made the change in her life, Desiree couldn't help but talk about her "blessings" book.

"Every morning I spend some time reading the Psalms," Desiree explained. "I can relate to all those emotional ups and downs. Then I write down everything I'm thankful for in my journal. If it's a tough morning, I go back and read what God has done for me in the past. That always brings to mind something new I need to say 'Thank You' for. Those few moments with God give me the courage to face the day with a positive outlook."

Consider a "blessings" book of your own. COUNTING YOUR BLESSINGS DIVIDES YOUR SORROW.

The LORD looks down and sees all mankind.

PSALM 33:13

Turn Yourself to me, and have mercy on me,
For I am desolate and afflicted.

PSALM 25:16 NKJV

We have this hope as an anchor for the soul,
firm and secure. It enters the inner sanctuary
behind the curtain, where Jesus, who went
before us, has entered on our behalf.

HEBREWS 6:19-20

Lost in the Crowd

College had never been part of Rhonda's grand scheme for life, but here she was. The only problem was she found the classrooms in college didn't feel as friendly as they had in high school. She felt alone, and invisible.

But she knew she wasn't. She knew God was by her side. She pictured Him walking beside her into class or sitting in the car with her as she drove to campus. The more she shared her heart with Him, the nearer she felt His presence.

Taking it one day at a time, Rhonda found herself making friends, and soon she fully enjoyed her new educational challenge. Moments spent with God each morning gave her the courage she needed to move on with her life.

Is there an unexpected challenge in your life? Reach out to God—He's always there for you.

COURAGE IS THE POWER TO LET GO OF THE FAMILIAR.

Whatever you do, do it all
for the glory of God.

1 CORINTHIANS 10:31

The lazy will not get what they want,
but those who work hard will.

PROVERBS 13:4 NCV

Whatever your hand finds to do,
do it with your might; for there is
no work or device or knowledge or
wisdom in the grave where you are going.

ECCLESIASTES 9:10 NKJV

EVERY CALLING IS GREAT
WHEN GREATLY PURSUED.

Just a Dishwasher

"Thanks a lot." Though he was smiling, the sarcasm dripped from Jason's lips nearly as heavily as the soapy water dripped off his apron. Three racks of dirty dishes blocked his exit from the kitchen. *This isn't the job I dreamed of,* he thought. *I wanted to make a difference.*

A baking pan slipped into the sink, splashing hot, sudsy water onto Jason's apron. He could feel it soaking through his clothes, but he continued to work. He scrubbed until the pots and pans were cleaner than they'd ever been.

"Jason," the kitchen manager said, "I just wanted to tell you how much I appreciate your attitude. You don't complain; you do good work and you make my day better. Thanks."

Jason paused for a moment and smiled. *With God's help, dishwashers can make a difference too,* he thought.

Are you doing your best, right where you are?

The unfolding of thy words gives light.

PSALM 119:130 RSV

I will delight in your principles
and not forget your word.

PSALM 119:16 NLT

In Him you also trusted, after you heard the
word of truth, the gospel of your salvation;
in whom also, having believed, you were
sealed with the Holy Spirit of promise.

EPHESIANS 1:13 NKJV

Discovery

Brian shuffled along the basement floor, flashlight darting left, then right. "I know it's here somewhere . . . " The circle of light stopped on a large chest. As soon as he opened it, the memories began to spill out.

Tears dripped from his eyes as he flipped through his sister's baby book. As he turned another page, his flashlight dropped into the chest and rolled against the back of the wooden box. The beam fixed on a black leather book.

Brian picked up Julia's Bible and dusted it off. He sadly recalled the last and only time he'd joined his sister at church: her funeral. He carefully replaced the baby book and closed the chest. As he reached the stairs, he wondered if the Bible would shed some light on his world. By the time he reached the main floor, he was counting on it.

Is there a Bible in your home that needs to be dusted off?

THE BIBLE IS A LIGHT YOU CAN SEE IN BOTH THE DARKEST NIGHTS AND THE BRIGHTEST DAYS.

God's voice thunders in marvelous ways; he
does great things beyond our understanding.

JOB 37:5

Give me understanding, and I shall
keep Your law; Indeed, I shall
observe it with my whole heart.

PSALM 119:34 NKJV

Give me understanding, and I shall
keep Your law; Indeed, I shall
observe it with my whole heart.

May the Lord lead you into a greater
understanding of God's love and the
endurance that is given by Christ.

2 THESSALONIANS 3:5 TEV

A Question of Perspective

Watching her nieces and nephews grow reminded Sarah of what it was like to be a small child herself—always asking questions. "Why is the grass green?" "Why don't fish drown?" "Why is thunder so loud?" As a teen, Sarah was beginning to realize there were some questions she would never have the answers to, like, "Did life just begin by accident?" "What happened to my mom after she died?" "Does what I do really make any difference in this world?"

When a friend mentioned to her that the Bible had some of the answers she was looking for, Sarah began to read. She was surprised to find not only answers, but also a reason for living.

There were still things she didn't understand; but the more Sarah learned about God, the more she trusted that He knew every answer.

A few moments in the Bible can bring peace to your heart and joy to your life as well.

OTHER BOOKS WERE GIVEN FOR OUR INFORMATION; THE BIBLE WAS GIVEN FOR OUR TRANSFORMATION.

You have made known to me the path of life;
you will fill me with joy in your presence,
with eternal pleasures at your right hand.

PSALM 16:11

Make me walk in the path of Your
commandments, for I delight in it.

PSALM 119:35 NASB

Thine ears shall hear a word behind thee, saying,
This is the way, walk ye in it, when ye turn to
the right hand, and when ye turn to the left.

ISAIAH 30:21 KJV

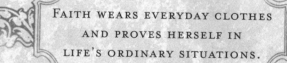

FAITH WEARS EVERYDAY CLOTHES
AND PROVES HERSELF IN
LIFE'S ORDINARY SITUATIONS.

A New Road

Amid the party horns, music, and laughter, Jeanie looked back over the past three years. Though her friends insisted on telling and retelling the story of her first time at the youth group—and what became known as "The Great Ketchup Event"—Jeanie's recollection landed on the morning *before* she attended.

It was a Sunday, and Jeanie sat where she always sat on Sunday mornings—on a cold, hard pew with her family in church. But this Sunday had been different. For the first time in her life, she really "got it." She understood this "God thing," as she'd referred to it so many times before. And what a change it made! It was a beginning and a direction she never would have anticipated.

As she blew out the candles on the cake, Jeanie silently thanked God that she'd seen the signpost that said, "This way."

God wants to be involved in the everyday moments of your life. Will you let Him?

In the image of God has God made man.

GENESIS. 9:6

Those who believe without seeing
me will be truly happy.

JOHN 20:29 NCV

The eyes of the Lord are on the righteous,
and His ears are open to their cry.

PSALM 34:15 NKJV

When No One Is Looking

At last count, Amanda had witnessed seventeen acts of what she called "minor deceit"—customers who broke an item and quietly slipped it back into place without reporting the incident to a store clerk. In fact, in the two years she'd worked at the mall gift shop, only one customer had honestly stepped forward. That young man, Mike, was now her boyfriend.

"Excuse me. I accidentally knocked this figurine off the shelf, and I'd like to pay for it." Those had been his first words to her. Before Mike, Amanda's relationships with guys always ended in disappointment and deception. But he was different; he was a man of integrity.

On their six-month dating anniversary he gave her the broken figurine, which had since been carefully glued together to look nearly new. She hadn't noticed before, but the figure looked a lot like her—especially the smile.

How do *you* handle those minor indiscretions when you think no one is looking?

IMAGE ISN'T
EVERYTHING;
INTEGRITY IS.

All who humble themselves before the
Lord shall be given every blessing,
and shall have wonderful peace.

PSALM 37:11 TLB

—

"Happy are those who are humble; they will
receive what God has promised!"

MATTHEW 5:5 TEV

—

When you do things, do not let selfishness or
pride be your guide. Instead, be humble and
give more honor to others than to yourselves.

PHILIPPIANS 2:3 NCV

—

Curtain Call

Without a word, Leah turned and headed back to the dressing room. She'd seen the cast list. *Another part as an extra,* she thought. Bitter tears coursed down her cheeks. She'd been the lead in the high school play last year, the main soloist in the choir, always first choice for any performance. Now, with the new drama coach, she struggled for small roles.

Angrily, Leah told God, "It's so unfair. My talent is wasted on these small roles. I *deserve* more." But as God's peace came over her, she also glimpsed His perspective—how any talent she had was a gift from Him, and how her hurt stemmed from pride, not injustice. In a few God moments, Leah found herself in need of forgiveness—as well as strength and inspiration to do the best she could with the part she had been given.

Ground is *never* lost when you commit yourself to God.

> TALENT IS
> GOD-GIVEN;
> BE THANKFUL.
> CONCEIT IS
> SELF-GIVEN;
> BE CAREFUL.

Dear friends, let us love one another, for love comes from God. Everyone who loves has been born of God and knows God.

1 JOHN 4:7

It is my prayer that your love may abound more and more, with knowledge and all discernment, so that you may approve what is excellent, and may be pure and blameless for the day of Christ.

PHILIPPIANS 1:9-10 RSV

Hope maketh not ashamed; because the love of God is shed abroad in our hearts by the Holy Ghost which is given unto us.

ROMANS 5:5 KJV

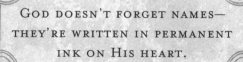

GOD DOESN'T FORGET NAMES—
THEY'RE WRITTEN IN PERMANENT
INK ON HIS HEART.

Known

In the back row of the classroom, Tim stared at the clock. The second hand moved like molasses. Tim hated school—well, not completely. He didn't mind the work, and the teachers were pretty good. In fact, school wouldn't be bad at all if it weren't for the other students.

He despised the name-calling, but he hated being ignored by everyone else even more. His dad would say, "I know it hurts, Tim," then share some story from his own high school days. "It may not seem like much comfort now, but you are important to God. He knows your name."

Suddenly the clock's rhythm was interrupted by the teacher's voice saying, " . . . and Tim aced this test. Nice work."

For that brief moment, everyone knew my name, Tim thought. *And I'm sure Dad is right; God has known it all along.*

You can be sure that God knows your name as well.

God is the strength of my heart
and my portion forever.

PSALM 73:26

Be kindly affectionate to one another
with brotherly love, in honor giving
preference to one another.

ROMANS 12:10 NKJV

Love suffers long and is kind; love does
not envy; love does not parade itself,
is not puffed up . . . Love never fails.

1 CORINTHIANS 13:4, 8 NKJV

The Challenge

Loving the unlovable is quite a challenge. You've been there before—perhaps at school, when that creepy classmate lied his way out of detention and wound up sitting right next to you. Now you get to hear his foul language first hand. Maybe you faced the challenge at the convenience store, when another customer bullied her way in front of you at the checkout line.

It's easy to love people who treat you respectfully. It's easy to love people who are patient, kind, and polite. It's easy to love people who smile. But the mean ones, the rude ones, the hopeless ones—now that's a different story.

In your own power, loving the unlovable comes out looking a lot like pity. Thankfully, God has a great reserve of pure love, and you can tap into it anytime you have a need.

YOUR HEART HAS MORE SPACE FOR LOVE WHEN IT'S FILLED BY GOD.

I lift my eyes to the hills—where does my help
come from? My help comes from the LORD,
the Maker of heaven and earth.

PSALM 121:1-2

≈

Trust God from the bottom of your heart;
don't try to figure out everything on your
own. Listen for God's voice in everything
you do, everywhere you go; he's the
one who will keep you on track.

PROVERBS 3:5-6 THE MESSAGE

≈

The LORD will guide you continually.

ISAIAH 58:11 NKJV

≈

Inner Battles

It sounded so simple. To lose weight, you need to eat less and exercise more. But Abby had struggled with her weight all her life. Even in grammar school, her mom bought her clothes from the "big girl" section. And the teasing certainly didn't help. Blame it on metabolism, poor eating habits, lousy genes, or just lack of self-control, all Abby knew was that she'd tried every new diet that came her way—without success.

She gave up dieting. Instead of counting fat grams and calories, she began to pray before she ate. She simply asked for God's wisdom and self-control. Soon Abby found herself turning down seconds and often choosing a piece of fruit over a bag of chips. Her weight loss wasn't dramatic, but it became consistent. Abby found that prayer worked.

No matter what challenge you are facing, God is ready to help.

THE TOUGHEST BATTLES WE FIGHT IN LIFE ARE OFTEN WITH OURSELVES.

A sweet friendship refreshes the soul.

PROVERBS 27:9 THE MESSAGE

There are "friends" who destroy each other,
but a real friend sticks closer than a brother.

PROVERBS 18:24 NLT

We love because he first loved us. If anyone says,
"I love God," yet hates his brother, he is a liar.
For anyone who does not love his brother, whom
he has seen, cannot love God, whom he has
not seen. And he has given us this command:
Whoever loves God must also love his brother.

1 JOHN 4:19-21

TRUE FRIENDSHIP IS ONE OF
GOD'S MOST PRECIOUS GIFTS.

Hands of Friendship

Katy finished her homework and stared out the window at the trees, their strong boughs lifted to the sky. Immediately she thought of Jeff. Mostly, she thought of his hands. They were strong hands, to be certain. He'd helped her family move three times—carrying her heavy dresser up three flights of stairs for the most recent change of address.

They were gentle hands too. Hands that surrounded Katy with a hug after her father died. Hands that prepared and brought her a meal when she was recovering from the flu. And they were capable hands. Hands that fixed a broken bicycle, and played beautiful music on a guitar.

A knock on the door roused Katy from her daydream. She walked over and peeked through the peephole. She laughed aloud at the distorted image of Jeff's hands covering his face. Katy smiled. *Those are the hands of a true friend*, she thought.

Take time today to thank God for the true friends He's placed in your life.

The heavens declare the glory of God;
the skies proclaim the work of his hands.

PSALM 19:1

Stop and consider God's wonders.
Do you know how God controls the clouds
and makes his lightning flash? Do you
know how the clouds hang poised, those
wonders of him who is perfect in knowledge?

JOB 37:14-16

Before the mountains were created,
before you made the earth and the world,
you are God, without beginning or end.

PSALM 90:2 NLT

Don't Miss the Miracles

Dad had that look in his eyes. Bobby loved his dad's impromptu celebrations. He'd wake the kids in the middle of the night, bundle them up in old sleeping bags, and then take everyone out to the backyard to watch a meteor shower. He'd interrupt dinner for a sunset or turn off the TV mid-program to redirect everyone's attention to the lightning flashing over the mountains. He'd halt a family hike to watch a line of ants carry leaves three times their size across the path. But, no matter what natural wonder happened to be taking place, his dad always said the same thing—"Thank you, God!"

Pausing to appreciate a work of art in a museum is a natural response to creativity and beauty. So is taking time to appreciate the incredible world God has made. His handiwork is everywhere. Today, why not take a walk or a drive in search of often-overlooked miracles?

> THE GALLERY OF GOD'S WONDERS IS ALWAYS OPEN AND NEVER CHARGES ADMISSION.

"Freely you have received, freely give."

MATTHEW 10:8

Forgive us the wrongs we have done, as we
forgive the wrongs that others have done to us.

MATTHEW 6:12 TEV

Be kind and compassionate to
one another, forgiving each other,
just as in Christ God forgave you.

EPHESIANS 4:32

Transforming Grace

"Come on, come on, come on . . . change!" Morgan muttered at the stoplight, but to no avail. The longer he sat in traffic, the more he saw red—not just in the obstinate light overhead. He was edgy about being late for class, but more than that, he was irritated by yet another argument with his dad.

"Change, now!" he yelled at the unyielding light. He was startled by the anger he felt, especially when he realized he really wanted to yell those words at his dad. That's when the thought suddenly occurred to him: *I wonder how many times God's wanted to yell those same words at me?*

When times get tough in relationships, it's easier to extend love to others when you recall how far God went to extend His love to you. Forgive and be forgiven—it's the highest expression of love.

FORGIVENESS IS A FUNNY THING—IT WARMS THE HEART AND COOLS THE STING.

You have freed me from my chains.

PSALM 116:16

The only temptation that has come to you is that which everyone has. But you can trust God, who will not permit you to be tempted more than you can stand. But when you are tempted, he will also give you a way to escape so that you will be able to stand it.

1 CORINTHIANS 10:13 NCV

Sin is no longer your master, for you are no longer subject to the law, which enslaves you to sin. Instead, you are free by God's grace.

ROMANS 6:14 NLT

WE CANNOT SAY NO TO
TEMPTATION WITHOUT SAYING YES
TO SOMETHING FAR BETTER.

Worth the Fight

Tony's announcement that he was leaving the ministry stunned the congregation. How could their youth pastor be addicted to pornography? As Peter listened from the third row, he stared uncomfortably at his own shoes and thought, *How soon until someone discovers my secret, as well?*

It was those e-mails he kept receiving. The ones marked XXX. At first he'd opened one by mistake. As for the rest, well, he rationalized "just looking" really didn't hurt anything. *But it sure seemed to have hurt Tony,* Peter reasoned. *Lord, help me,* he prayed to himself. *I don't know what to do to stop.*

The first step to battling any addiction is admitting there's a battle. Is there any area in your life that is increasingly out of your control? Ask God for help, but don't stop there. Confess what you're doing to a trusted friend or counselor who'll hold you accountable. Get the help you need, even if it's difficult or embarrassing. It's a battle worth winning.

The LORD is good, a refuge in times of
trouble. He cares for those who trust in him.

NAHUM 1:7

Yea, though I walk through the valley
of the shadow of death, I will fear no evil:
for thou art with me; thy rod and
thy staff they comfort me.

PSALM 23:4 KJV

The LORD is my light and the one who
saves me. I fear no one. The LORD
protects my life; I am afraid of no one.

PSALM 27:1 NCV

Next Gas, One Mile

Heath knew he was in trouble. The gauge had read "Full" for far too long to be accurate. Driving along an unknown stretch of highway on an empty tank was just asking for trouble. Just then, the engine sputtered, and the now-silent car sat on the side of the road just a few feet from a sign that read, "Next Gas, one mile."

Heath prayed for strength. Then he began walking and thanking God it was still light outside. As he continued along the empty road, he began to imagine all the terrible things that could happen to him. But then a few minutes later, he felt peace. "God is with me," he said with a smile only the birds and lizards could see.

God's promise to always be near trumped that fear moments before he reached the gas station.

Trust God, and the long walks won't seem so long— or so lonely.

FEAR KNOCKED
AT THE DOOR.
FAITH ANSWERED.
NO ONE
WAS THERE.

My chosen ones will have
satisfaction in their work.

ISAIAH 65:23 THE MESSAGE

I know the thoughts that I think toward you,
says the LORD, thoughts of peace and not
of evil, to give you a future and a hope.

JEREMIAH 29:11 NKJV

He has filled him with the Spirit of God,
with ability, with intelligence, with
knowledge, and with all craftsmanship.

EXODUS 35:31 RSV

Afloat

Were it not for the fact that his boat drifted farther and farther into the middle of the lake, Brad might have been enchanted by this moment. What could be better than a perfect foggy morning of fishing on a beautiful lake? But there was this little problem—he was out of gas, without oars.

In a few hours, the lake would teem with life above the waterline—*someone will see me,* he reasoned. Still, Brad couldn't seem to get rid of the knot in the pit of his stomach. How could he chase the anxiety away and enjoy his morning retreat?

Then he had an idea. *I wonder how many Scripture passages I can quote by heart,* he thought. Two hours later, he heard the familiar sound of an outboard motor. As he hooked up the tow rope, Brad decided he needed to do two things right away: stock his boat with oars *and* learn more Scripture.

SCRIPTURE IS FAR HIGHER AND WIDER THAN OUR NEED.

Your revelation is the tune I dance to.

PSALM 119:77 THE MESSAGE

You are the light of the world—like a city on a mountain, glowing in the night for all to see. Don't hide your light under a basket! Instead, put it on a stand and let it shine for all.

MATTHEW 5:14-15 NLT

We are His workmanship, created in Christ Jesus for good works, which God prepared beforehand that we should walk in them.

EPHESIANS 2:10 NKJV

ONLY GOD CAN PUT THE TOUCH ON SOMETHING WHICH CHANGES IT FROM THE COMMONPLACE TO SOMETHING SPECIAL, DIFFERENT, AND APART.

A Different Beat

The right place at the right time, doing the right thing—that's how Tony felt as he handed his bandmates copies of the song he'd written the night before. In the silence that passed while Pete the guitarist, Greg the bass player, and Marcos the lead singer read over the words, Tony prayed they'd want to know more about the message of the song.

"This is great! How did you come up with something this good?" they asked. "We didn't even know you could write."

"It's based on something I believe in," he responded.

Greg and Pete began to hammer out their parts, while Marcos came over to Tony. "I always knew you were a little different—so you're a Christian? That's cool. I used to go to church. Maybe we should talk."

"I'd like that," Tony answered, smiling.

Are you using your God-given talents to point your friends in the right direction?

You have turned for me my
mourning into dancing.

PSALM 30:11 NKJV

Let them praise His name with
the dance; let them sing praises
to Him with the timbrel and harp.

PSALM 149:3 NKJV

There is a time to cry and a time to laugh.
There is a time to be sad and a time to dance.

ECCLESIASTES 3:4 NCV

Get on Your Feet

It was time for the church offering—not a modern dance recital. But the music lifted Twila's heart so suddenly, she felt it could lift her out of her seat, as well. Wouldn't Mrs. Martinson, sitting next to her, just freak out? Twila smiled at the picture that came to mind and decided she'd wait until she got home. Then she would turn up the music and dance—with God.

Just as our words communicate with God, so do our actions. Some people kneel in adoration; some raise their hands in praise; some dance as a way of expressing emotions too deep for words. Dancing often conveys feelings of joy at celebrations. But dance can express countless emotions, including awe, happiness, sorrow, and even anger. God understands the language of the heart, no matter how it's expressed.

If music moves you, put on a song that draws you to God, and see where your feet take you.

THE WORSHIP OF GOD IS NOT A RULE OF SAFETY— IT IS AN ADVENTURE OF THE SPIRIT.

The LORD says, "Do not cling to events of the
past or dwell on what happened long ago.
Watch for the new thing I am going to do.
It is happening already—you can see it now!"

ISAIAH 43:18-19 TEV

Forgetting the past and looking forward
to what lies ahead, I strain to reach the
end of the race and receive the prize
for which God, through Christ Jesus,
is calling us up to heaven.

PHILIPPIANS 3:13-14 NLT

"Do not fear, for you will not be ashamed;
neither be disgraced, for you will
not be put to shame; for you will
forget the shame of your youth."

ISAIAH 54:4 NKJV

Take Out the Trash

The closet was empty, but Tracy's bedroom took on the appearance of a war zone. Boxes, papers, photographs, old music CDs, and odds and ends littered the floor. The memory shrapnel was overwhelming.

Then Tracy picked up a photo of her old boyfriend, Dean, and something unexpected tugged at her heart. She recalled the good times first, but soon was flooded with memories of his arrogance, the wild parties, and more than a closet full of her own mistakes.

An all-too-familiar emptiness began to seep into her heart—until she spied the blue box. It was the box she had filled with notes of encouragement after she walked away from Dean. It was the box that had built her friendship with God. Suddenly her floor wasn't filled with precious memories—just a bunch of trash and one very special blue box.

Have you been clinging to the past? Throw it away, and with God's help, move forward.

> THE PAST IS VALUABLE AS A GUIDEPOST, BUT DANGEROUS IF USED AS A HITCHING POST.

May the favor of the Lord our God rest upon us; establish the work of our hands for us.

PSALM 90:17

Jesus said to him, "If you want to be perfect, go, sell what you have and give to the poor, and you will have treasure in heaven; and come, follow Me."

MATTHEW 19:21 NKJV

My whole being will exclaim, "Who is like you, O LORD? You rescue the poor from those too strong for them, the poor and needy from those who rob them."

PSALM 35:10

CHARITY IS THE SCOPE OF ALL GOD'S COMMANDS.

Self-Service

Allison glanced at the line of bedraggled humanity—and sighed. She'd volunteered at the soup kitchen because a friend mentioned what a gratifying job it was. Gloria just found it tedious and depressing. Anyone could scoop spaghetti. Big deal.

"God bless you," someone said, and the words caused Allison to actually look at the person she was serving. There stood a young woman not much older than herself.

"Uh, you're welcome," Allison stuttered. Suddenly she felt hot with shame. God could turn anything, even the simple words of a homeless person, into a blessing. In a fleeting second, Allison prayed that God would use her time to bless others in any way He saw fit. Suddenly, the job didn't seem so tedious after all.

Working through your own power and in your own selfish motives works against success and blessing, not for it. Whatever you find yourself doing today, ask God to take your efforts and turn them into something more.

I praise you because I am fearfully
and wonderfully made.

PSALM 139:14

❧

Do not let your adornment be merely outward—
arranging the hair, wearing gold, or putting
on fine apparel—rather let it be the hidden
person of the heart, with the incorruptible
beauty of a gentle and quiet spirit, which
is very precious in the sight of God.

1 PETER 3:3-4 NKJV

❧

Why do you worry about clothes? See how the
lilies of the field grow. They do not labor or
spin. Yet I tell you that not even Solomon in
all his splendor was dressed like one of these.
If that is how God clothes the grass of the
field, which is here today and tomorrow is
thrown into the fire, will he not much more
clothe you, O you of little faith?

MATTHEW 6:28-30

❧

Comparison Shopping

Josie slid into her beanbag chair, feeling like she'd hit the jackpot. Today, the mailman had brought two fashion magazines and three new spring catalogs. Shopping while lazing in her favorite chair—could it get any better than this? She could browse for hours. *I'd really feel beautiful in this,* she thought as she gazed at an outfit on the glossy page.

Then she felt the nudge of God's voice inside. *You're already beautiful,* she felt Him saying. In an instant, Josie realized the real reason she wanted those clothes. She wanted to look like the model who was wearing them. She wanted her friends to notice. She had always believed that with just the right outfit, she'd finally be beautiful. But, somehow, she was beginning to understand that God had created her to be just who she was, no more and no less. In His eyes, she was already beautiful.

Do you struggle to feel beautiful? Look at yourself in God's mirror.

LET EACH MAN THINK HIMSELF AN ACT OF GOD, HIS MIND A THOUGHT OF GOD, HIS LIFE A BREATH OF GOD.

I'd sell off the whole world to get you back,
trade the creation just for you.

ISAIAH 43:4 THE MESSAGE

❧

I am convinced that neither death nor life,
neither angels nor demons, neither the present
nor the future, nor any powers, neither height
nor depth, nor anything else in all creation,
will be able to separate us from the love of
God that is in Christ Jesus our Lord.

ROMANS 8:38-39

❧

The Spirit is God's guarantee that he will give
us everything he promised and that he has
purchased us to be his own people.
This is just one more reason for
us to praise our glorious God.

EPHESIANS 1:14 NLT

❧

Rescue

It had all the makings of a great action film—some guy, sacrificing his own life to save his true love. Kara loved stories like that, but they always left her feeling sad and empty. *If only there was someone who would rescue me,* she usually thought.

But this time, the story she was hearing wasn't fiction. It was coming from a church pulpit. When Kara joined her friend Carl for his church's Easter service, she had expected to hear what a horrible person she was—that she had let God down and had better get her life together. Instead, she heard that Someone came to earth to rescue her. She heard that there really was a Hero who loved her. Kara knew she'd finally found what her heart had always longed for.

Do you long for a love that is true and lasting? God has already given His life for you, and He is waiting to claim you for His own.

IT IS NOT YOUR HOLD ON CHRIST THAT SAVES YOU, BUT HIS HOLD ON YOU!

Have you not heard? Long ago I ordained it.
In the days of old I planned it;
now I have brought it to pass.

ISAIAH 37:26

Thou dost show me the path of life; in
thy presence there is fulness of joy, in thy
right hand are pleasures for evermore.

PSALM 16:11 RSV

He set my feet on a rock and
gave me a firm place to stand.

PSALM 40:2

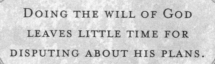

DOING THE WILL OF GOD
LEAVES LITTLE TIME FOR
DISPUTING ABOUT HIS PLANS.

A Bigger Picture

Do you ever wonder about the script God has written for your life? Weren't you supposed to be the all-star athlete or the prom queen? Didn't God mean for all your dreams to come true?

So why did you get the script that says, "You're going to fight with your mother, struggle to feel accepted, then slip on a patch of ice and break your arm"? Surely this is wrong.

Try this little experiment. Get out a beautiful picture; something from a magazine, perhaps. Take a large piece of paper and cover the whole picture. Carefully cut a hole half the size of a pencil eraser in the paper. Slide the hole around on top of the picture. What do you see? Not much? That's all we see of God's plan too. Maybe today's script isn't much fun, but God sees the bigger picture. You know—the beautiful one under the paper.

He satisfies the longing soul, and fills
the hungry soul with goodness.

PSALM 107:9 NKJV

Delight yourself also in the LORD, and He
shall give you the desires of your heart.

PSALM 37:4 NKJV

Praise be to the God and Father of our
Lord Jesus Christ, who has blessed us
in the heavenly realms with every
spiritual blessing in Christ.

EPHESIANS 1:3

Full

"What do you long for?" The small group leader had posed this same question twelve weeks earlier. Back then Terry had known exactly what to say. "I long for someone special to love, a chance to play my music, and enough money to live independently." Others had offered similar responses. But now, after all they'd studied and explored together, the answer wasn't so simple.

"I'm not quite sure what I long for," Terry began. "Perhaps it's a chance to know God more intimately." Others nodded, then added their insights. One thing was certain—he knew what longing was now. Those things he'd mentioned twelve weeks ago? Sure, he still dreamed of them; but his longing was for something deeper.

Your deepest longings are placed within you by God. They cannot be filled by a girlfriend or boyfriend, more time for your hobbies, or money. Only the Creator of the longing can truly fill it.

GOD IS NEVER FOUND ACCIDENTALLY.

I will grant peace in the land, and you will
lie down and no one will make you afraid.

LEVITICUS 26:6

He delivers me from my enemies. You also
lift me up above those who rise against me;
You have delivered me from the violent man.

PSALM 18:48 NKJV

My times are in Your hand; deliver me
from the hand of my enemies, and
from those who persecute me.

PSALM 31:15 NKJV

Battle Zone

The lion will lay down with the lamb. *Right. And Paul will apologize, tell his thugs to back off, and become my best friend,* Nick thought sarcastically. He wondered if he should wait a few more minutes before leaving the safety of the school building. Maybe Paul would give up and go home.

No way. There they were, standing at the end of the path, staring in Nick's direction. "Okay—okay—this is the part where you guys beat me up," Nick called out. "I know how it goes. Just get it over with, okay?"

Nick watched as Paul and his friends approached. "Beat you up? Nah. Me and my buddies decided to let you off easy," Paul said. Nick waited for the punch line—or the punch. Neither came. As Paul and his buddies walked away, Nick paused to thank God for turning a lion's roar into a soft purr.

WHEN WE HAVE NOTHING LEFT BUT GOD, THEN WE BECOME AWARE THAT GOD IS ENOUGH.

Ask where the good way is, and walk in it,
and you will find rest for your souls.

JEREMIAH 6:16

Lead me in the right path, O LORD, or my
enemies will conquer me. Tell me clearly
what to do, and show me which way to turn.

PSALM 5:8 NLT

The true children of God are those
who let God's Spirit lead them.

ROMANS 8:14 NCV

THERE'S NO BETTER
COMPASS FOR LIFE THAN
GOD AND HIS WORD.

Road to Nowhere

Blaine was no longer just edgy. He was well over the edge. He knew the turnoff was around here somewhere, but the pouring rain was either obstructing the street sign or had washed it away all together. As he drove by the same convenience store for the third time, it crossed his mind that he should go in and ask for directions. His girlfriend would if she were here, but she wasn't. Blaine turned the windshield wipers up another notch and kept driving down the same road, not any closer to his destination than he had been an hour ago.

The idea that real men don't ask for directions is a stereotype that has been passed down in our society. In reality, regardless of gender, asking God for direction is something we should do every day—sometimes every moment. And remember, directions are useless unless we follow them.

Do you need direction for your life? Don't hesitate! God is willing and able to point you in the way you should go.

Know that the LORD is God. It is he
who made us, and we are his; we are
his people, the sheep of his pasture.

PSALM 100:3

In your unfailing love you will lead the people
you have redeemed. In your strength you
will guide them to your holy dwelling.

EXODUS 15:13

We humans keep brainstorming options
and plans, but God's purpose prevails.

PROVERBS 19:21 THE MESSAGE

Smiling Down

From an early age, Tina had known she was going to be someone special. At first, she was going to wear ballet slippers and dance on a huge stage in front of an adoring audience. Later, she was certain she'd be the first woman president. Then she decided to become a famous author one day.

But things changed. Tina stopped making her own plans and instead asked God to direct her steps and make her life fruitful. Soon after, she landed a part-time job working for a local youth organization. The pay wasn't great—the accolades few. She didn't have a stage, but she did have a platform for influencing the lives of children. As she led the children to write essays about themselves, she realized her writing talents were being used after all. Tina was someone special. She had found her purpose in life.

In God's eyes, you are just as special. And if you ask Him, He will do for you what He did for Tina.

THE ENGINEER OF THE UNIVERSE HAS MADE ME PART OF HIS WHOLE DESIGN.

Whatever is true, whatever is noble, whatever is right, whatever is pure, whatever is lovely, whatever is admirable—if anything is excellent or praiseworthy—think about such things.

PHILIPPIANS 4:8

I will have nothing to do with evil.

PSALM 101:4

Friends, I'd say you'll do best by filling your minds and meditating on things true, noble, reputable, authentic, compelling, gracious— the best, not the worst; the beautiful, not the ugly; things to praise, not things to curse. Put into practice what you learned from me, what you heard and saw and realized. Do that, and God, who makes everything work together, will work you into his most excellent harmonies.

PHILIPPIANS 4:8-9 THE MESSAGE

Food for Thought

Shelly munched on popcorn and chatted with her friends while they waited for the movie to start. She didn't know much about the plot, but when her friends from school invited her to the theater, she had jumped at the chance. After a grueling week at school, she was ready for a little fun.

It wasn't long after the opening credits that Shelly started to feel uncomfortable. She couldn't figure out whether the sex, the violence, or the language was the most offensive. But she was sure of one thing—she needed to leave. "I'll meet you in the lobby," she whispered to her friends. When she got out into the light, she was surprised to see Christina right behind her.

"I'm so glad you left when you did," Christina said. "I was too embarrassed to do it alone."

Garbage in, garbage out— what's true for your computer goes for your mind as well.

MAN'S MIND IS THE HOLY OF HOLIES, AND TO ADMIT EVIL THOUGHTS IS LIKE SETTING UP AN IDOL IN THE TEMPLE.

The LORD longs to be gracious to you.

ISAIAH 30:18

Therefore, since through God's mercy we have
this ministry, we do not lose heart. Rather, we
have renounced secret and shameful ways; we
do not use deception, nor do we distort the
word of God. On the contrary, by setting
forth the truth plainly we commend ourselves
to every man's conscience in the sight of God.

2 CORINTHIANS 4:1-2

The true Light that gives light to
all was coming into the world!

JOHN 1:9 NCV

OUR GOD HAS A BIG ERASER.

Finding Forgiveness

Leigh had never felt she was really doing anything wrong. But now, after getting to know God, she saw her actions in a different light; and it wasn't a very flattering picture. Countless times she'd gone to God and apologized, but she never felt "clean." Her friends from the youth group talked about the blessings God brought their way, but Leigh felt as though she deserved nothing. Instead, it seemed as if she'd be paying God back for the rest of her life.

Then she met Mark. He loved her in spite of her past. Through him, Leigh caught a glimpse of what unconditional love and forgiveness were all about. She'd finally found a place of acceptance with God.

Once you've asked God for forgiveness, you're clean in His eyes, no matter how you feel.

Happy are those whose strength comes
from you, who want to travel to Jerusalem.

PSALM 84:5 NCV

Help us, O God our Savior, for the
glory of your name; deliver us and
forgive our sins for your name's sake.

PSALM 79:9

"Why do you look at the speck of
sawdust in your brother's eye and pay no
attention to the plank in your own eye?"

MATTHEW 7:3

Repeat Offender

"If brains were dynamite, she wouldn't have enough to blow her nose!" Kristi remarked. Her comment about the new girl elicited laughter from everyone at the lunch table, but as soon as she'd said it, Kristi mentally kicked herself.

Just this morning, she'd talked to God about how her sarcasm was getting out of control. She tried not to cut others down, but some people just left themselves wide open—or so she rationalized. But here it was, barely noon, and Kristi was apologizing again. "Okay, God," she prayed. "This is it! I'm going to quit cutting people down or die trying!"

The truth is, everyone's going to die trying. Trying to change ingrained habits or dysfunctional behavior is an ongoing process, even when you're leaning on God's strength for help. Don't beat yourself up when you fail. God extends grace and forgiveness, not a paddle and a dunce cap.

MAN IS BORN BROKEN. HE LIVES BY MENDING. THE GRACE OF GOD IS GLUE.

The people walking in darkness
have seen a great light.

ISAIAH 9:2

In him was life, and that life was the light
of men. The light shines in the darkness,
but the darkness has not understood it.

JOHN 1:4-5

You are not like that, for you are a chosen
people. You are a kingdom of priests, God's
holy nation, his very own possession. This is
so you can show others the goodness of God,
for he called you out of the darkness
into his wonderful light.

1 PETER 2:9 NLT

Blinded by the Light

"I can't see! Where did you go?"

"I'm right in front of you. Just follow the little red light." A tiny laser pointer dot appeared at Jordan's feet. Little by little, Caitlin led Jordan through the pitch-black room. She had already completed the maze a half-dozen times.

"That is the strangest experience I've ever had," said Jordan as he and Caitlin stepped through the door into the lobby of the renovated theater. "I just paid five bucks to freak myself out."

"Want to try it again?"

Halfway through the maze this time, the lights suddenly came on. Jordan and Caitlin were temporarily blinded. When they could finally see, they discovered the maze wasn't nearly as frightening as it had been in the dark.

When you've spent a lifetime in darkness, it can take a little while to get used to the light of God. But when your eyes finally adjust, you will find that life isn't quite so scary anymore.

DARKNESS IS MY POINT OF VIEW, MY RIGHT TO MYSELF; LIGHT IS GOD'S POINT OF VIEW.

He will be the sure foundation for your times, a rich store of salvation and wisdom and knowledge; the fear of the LORD is the key to this treasure.

ISAIAH 33:6

Do not be wise in your own eyes;
fear the LORD, and turn away from evil.

PROVERBS 3:7 NRSV

God chose the foolish things of the world to shame the wise; God chose the weak things of the world to shame the strong. He chose the lowly things of this world and the despised things— and the things that are not—to nullify the things that are, so that no one may boast before him.

1 CORINTHIANS 1:27-29

KNOWLEDGE IS HORIZONTAL.
WISDOM IS VERTICAL—
IT COMES DOWN FROM ABOVE.

Wise Up

Kyle and his parents viewed anything less than straight A's unthinkable, any status less than valedictorian, unacceptable. "Average" was not a word Kyle could relate to. He grew up believing he was a step above the ordinary, which made it easy to look down on those around him.

Then a friend, whose IQ happened to be even higher than his own, introduced Kyle to a God who valued wisdom over intelligence and compassion over knowledge. That glimpse of God's character turned Kyle's world upside down because he discovered he was no longer on top. But, at the same time, he'd never felt more valued or more challenged by the mysteries of life that lay before him.

Intelligence and faith are not only compatible, but also complementary. What do you do with what you learn about God? Is your spiritual life more like an intellectual exercise or a growing relationship?

Where the Spirit of the Lord is,
there is freedom.

2 CORINTHIANS 3:17

Christ has really set us free. Now make
sure that you stay free, and don't get
tied up again in slavery to the law.

GALATIANS 5:1 NLT

"If you hold to my teaching, you are really
my disciples. Then you will know the truth,
and the truth will set you free."

JOHN 8:31-32

Finally Free

"Religion is just a bunch of rules designed for people who can't live without them," Shawn had always said. And Shawn hated rules. He liked purple hair, speaking his mind, and eating brownies for breakfast. He was convinced he had no use for God, until one day when he found himself drawn to a "rule breaker" like himself.

This man worked on Sundays when all the religious people said He shouldn't. He hung out with people with bad reputations. He made grown-ups wait while He spent time with kids. And He wouldn't stay dead. Most radical of all, He didn't say, "Change, and then I'll love you." He said, "I love you the way you are."

When Shawn met Jesus Christ, he found himself beginning to change— not his purple hair—but his heart.

Following God is not synonymous with following a set of religious rules. It's more like a heart makeover that sets you free to be who you really are.

> RELIGION OFFERS RULES; GOD OFFERS RELATIONSHIP.

In Your presence is fullness of joy.

PSALM 16:11 NKJV

Great is his faithfulness; his mercies
begin afresh each day.

LAMENTATIONS 3:23 NLT

I'm going to do a brand new thing.
See, I have already begun!

ISAIAH 43:19 TLB

Quiet Timezzzzzz

Tina took her Bible off the shelf, just as she did every morning. She tried never to miss her quiet time, but lately she had realized something was missing. Every word she read seemed boring, every prayer repetitive. God seemed millions of miles away. She sighed, read a chapter, then left the room, unchanged.

Suppose someone wanted to spend time with you every day. Now, suppose you went to the same place, did the same things, and had the same conversation over and over again. Boring, huh? Why put your relationship with God in this same type of a box?

Shake things up a bit. Write God a letter. Just sit and listen. Take a walk. Take a bath. Sing a song. Use a Bible commentary. Read a book on prayer. Write your own psalm. Talk to God aloud. Just don't give up. He loves you more than you know, and He wants to be part of your life, not just your routine.

LET YOUR RELIGION BE LESS OF A THEORY AND MORE OF A LOVE AFFAIR.

Follow God's example in everything you do
just as a much loved child imitates his father.

EPHESIANS 5:1 TLB

We do not want you to become lazy, but
to imitate those who through faith and
patience inherit what has been promised.

HEBREWS 6:12

"I have set you an example that you should
do as I have done for you. I tell you the truth,
no servant is greater than his master, nor is
a messenger greater than the one who sent
him. Now that you know these things,
you will be blessed if you do them."

JOHN 13:15-17

NO MAN DOETH WELL BUT
GOD HATH PART IN HIM.

Follow the Leader

Some say that dogs resemble their masters. (Or is it, people resemble their dogs?) If you hang around with the wrong crowd, you'll eventually end up being one of them. In other words, you grow to resemble those you spend the most time with.

Just look at a high school campus. Some teens imitate others intentionally, whether it's with hairstyles, slang, or piercing yet another body part. But after a while, unintentional imitation begins to take place as well—speech patterns, body language, and attitude. That's why your parents want you to hang out with the "right crowd."

It's also one more reason why "hanging out" with God should be the top priority in your life. Who better to look to for an example? Whose habits would you rather adopt, intentionally or otherwise? Take a look at your life. In what ways are you growing to resemble your heavenly Father?

Your path led through the sea, your way
through the mighty waters, though
your footprints were not seen.

PSALM 77:19

≋

This poor man cried out, and the LORD heard
him, and saved him out of all his troubles.

PSALM 34:6 NKJV

≋

He comes alongside us when we go through
hard times, and before you know it, he brings
us alongside someone else who is going
through hard times so that we can be there
for that person just as God was there for us.

2 CORINTHIANS 1:4 THE MESSAGE

≋

Rising Tides

The perfect shell sat half buried in a small pile of rocks, its spiral silhouette unbroken by the pounding surf. Jeremy picked it up and dusted off the sticky grains of sand. Although he walked this beach every morning, a shell like this was a rare find. The shore was littered with bits of shell, coral, and smoothly sanded glass, but the rocks and the fierceness of the sea deposited most of its treasures here in pieces.

What a journey this shell must have had, Jeremy thought. He couldn't help but think of his own rocky journey over the past few years. He could finally look back on it and see how God had brought him through, unbroken. Jeremy put the shell in his pocket, a reminder of God's faithfulness through the storms of life.

What can you do to remember God's faithfulness when you can't see Him clearly during difficult times?

WHEN OUTWARD STRENGTH IS BROKEN, FAITH RESTS ON THE PROMISES.

When I awake in heaven, I will be fully
satisfied, for I will see you face to face.

PSALM 17:15 TLB

≈

May the LORD, the God of Israel,
under whose wings you have come
to take refuge, reward you fully.

RUTH 2:12 NLT

≈

Without faith it is impossible to please Him,
for he who comes to God must believe
that He is, and that He is a rewarder
of those who diligently seek Him.

HEBREWS 11:6 NKJV

≈

Innocent Obsession

Dark, light, truffle, solid, or filled—Alicia wasn't particularly choosy about her obsession, just as long as it was chocolate. She kept a box hidden in her locker at school, one in her dresser drawer at home, and one in the closet for emergencies.

It was only 8:30 in the morning, but Alicia already felt overwhelmed by what the day held for her: two tests and a difficult rehearsal to get through in band practice. She reached for her secret stash, then stopped. She knew she turned to chocolate when she was depressed, tired, frustrated, lonely, or stressed. *Maybe I should reach for something that could actually change the way I'm feeling,* she speculated. Then she bowed her head and took a few moments to ask God for His help.

What do you turn to when life becomes a struggle? What do you reach for to fill the emptiness inside? Remember, a glimpse of God's presence is better than the finest chocolate.

PRAYER IS TOTALLY FAT-FREE.

Faith is being sure of what we hope for
and certain of what we do not see.

HEBREWS 11:1

Those who know your name will trust
in you, for you, LORD, have never
forsaken those who seek you.

PSALM 9:10

See, God has come to save me! I will
trust and not be afraid, for the Lord is
my strength and song; he is my salvation.

ISAIAH 12:2 TLB

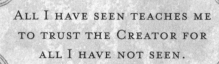

ALL I HAVE SEEN TEACHES ME
TO TRUST THE CREATOR FOR
ALL I HAVE NOT SEEN.

Your Father's Eyes

You don't need to be an optometrist to know that God's eyes are not the same as yours. They witnessed the creation of the world. They watched you as you were formed in your mother's womb. They can look straight into your heart.

That's where faith comes in. To begin to see things through God's eyes, you first have to grow to trust His heart. Like any relationship, trust builds over time. But it's put to the test when you believe God loves you, yet circumstances seem to scream the exact opposite. That's when you need to remember you don't have the ability to see every situation through God-colored glasses. You can only see the present and the past, while God can look ahead to the future.

Is there any circumstance in your life that makes you doubt God really has your best interest in mind? What is the best reassurance that He does?

The LORD your God has arrived to live among you. He is a mighty savior. He will rejoice over you with great gladness. With his love, he will calm all your fears. He will exult over you by singing a happy song.

ZEPHANIAH 3:17 NLT

He protected us on our entire journey.

JOSHUA 24:17

The LORD watches over all who love him.

PSALM 145:20 NRSV

Close Call

Gail had only had her driver's license for eight weeks. Out of the corner of her eye, she saw the blur of a red truck. In a split second, she realized it was going to run the light. As the words, "God, no!" escaped from her lips, everything seemed to move in slow motion—Gail hitting the brakes; her car straining to stop; and the truck, swerving, missing her by inches, then speeding down the road as if nothing had happened. Her heart raced as she pulled over to the curb to catch her breath.

While her adrenaline still pumped wildly, Gail found herself amazed—and thankful—that she was alive and unhurt. It was a blessing she'd taken for granted just moments before, and now she was filled with a renewed appreciation for how precious life was, and how fragile. As she pulled back onto the road, her heart couldn't stop giving thanks for her mother's constant prayer for God to watch over the newest driver in the family.

How has God's protection touched your life today?

BEING PRAYERFUL IS AS IMPORTANT AS BEING CAREFUL.

The plans of the LORD stand firm forever, the purposes of his heart through all generations.

PSALM 33:11

"I make known the end from the beginning, from ancient times, what is still to come. I say: My purpose will stand, and I will do all that I please."

ISAIAH 46:10

"I know that You can do everything, and that no purpose of Yours can be withheld from You."

JOB 42:2 NKJV

Divine Design

The movie was about to start. Jill hurried to the women's restroom, not wanting to miss a moment of the three-hour epic ahead of her. After washing her hands, she hurriedly reached above her head for a towel. Instantly, water from her wet hands rolled down her wrists and into the sleeves of her baggy sweater. "Who were these things designed for, the LA Lakers?" she muttered. "You'd think someone designing a bathroom would have figured out the benefits of reaching *down* for a towel, instead of up!"

As she made her way back to her seat, Jill laughed at herself and shared a brief moment with God. *It's a good thing that You put more thought into Your plans than people do! You didn't make the world on a whim, did You?*

No. God's plans unfold always at a perfect pace with an understanding of your past, present, and future. You can be certain of that.

THE BLUEPRINTS OF LIFE WERE DRAWN BY A HEART OF LOVE.

The unfolding of your words gives light;
it gives understanding to the simple.

PSALM 119:130

His powerful Word is sharp as a surgeon's scalpel,
cutting through everything, whether doubt
or defense, laying us open to listen and obey.
Nothing and no one is impervious to God's
Word. We can't get away from it—no matter what.

HEBREWS 4:12-13 THE MESSAGE

Let the word of Christ dwell in you richly as you
teach and admonish one another with all wisdom,
and as you sing psalms, hymns and spiritual
songs with gratitude in your hearts to God.

COLOSSIANS 3:16

AN OPEN BIBLE IN THE HAND
IS WORTH TWO ON THE SHELF.

Picture Perfect

Ricky didn't care if the glasses looked ridiculous; he wasn't about to miss any of the 3-D movie marathon. He and his friends put on their plastic shades and waited for the action to start. As a space-ship seemed to dart right into the middle of the ducking audience, Ricky couldn't help but take a peek at the movie without his glasses.

The magic was gone. The picture was nothing more than a jumble of blurry lines over the original photo-graphic image. It reminded him of what his youth pastor had said last night—reading the Bible was like putting on 3-D glasses. Without your Bible "glasses," life looks pretty confusing; but when you look at things through God's eyes, it all makes sense.

Do you have your Bible "glasses" on? It makes life a lot more fun.

May he give you the desire of your heart
and make all your plans succeed.

PSALM 20:4

Give your entire attention to what God is
doing right now, and don't get worked up
about what may or may not happen tomorrow.

MATTHEW 6:34 THE MESSAGE

Be delighted with the Lord. Then he
will give you all your heart's desires.
Commit everything you do to the Lord.
Trust him to help you do it and he will.

PSALM 37:4-5 TLB

Perfect Gifts

"Cosmic kill-joy"—that's what Shelby called God. Believing God existed was one thing; putting her life in His hands was quite another. "God wants prune-faced missionaries, not classical cellists," she had convinced herself.

After months of struggling to keep her grades up without abandoning her music, Shelby finally gave up. More out of desperation than love or commitment, she prayed, "Okay, God, You win. If You want me to give up the cello, I'll do it. You know I'm afraid to say this, but please lead me where You want me to go."

To her surprise, God didn't lead her away from her music. Instead, when she took her nephew to his piano lessons, she stepped into a glimpse of God's new direction for her life—a children's program was looking for someone to teach the cello after school. And the lesson times coordinated perfectly with her homework schedule.

When you surrender your dreams to God, you will be squarely on the road to fulfilling them.

THE ONLY GIFT GOD GIVES THAT EVER NEEDS TO BE RETURNED IS HIS LOVE.

We know that all things work together
for good to those who love God.

ROMANS 8:28 NKJV

We will be our guide, even unto death.

PSALM 48:14 KJV

You will keep on guiding me all my life with
your wisdom and counsel; and afterwards
receive me into the glories of heaven!

PSALM 73:24 TLB

Life Supreme

"What do you want on your pizza?" Sandra called from the kitchen. Her girlfriends—all five of them—had agreed to a "movie madness" sleepover as long as there was plenty of pizza.

"Everything!" a couple of them said.

"Just cheese on mine," another girl called out.

"Pepperoni!" the others cried.

Sandra laughed and clarified their order. "Okay, one pepperoni, one cheese, and one with everything. Even anchovies?"

"No way," they shouted.

"Didn't think so," Sandra said. "How about some wood glue with that mozzarella? How about a little grass?" Her friends laughed. "You mean you don't want *everything* on your pizza?"

God says He'll work everything together for good in our lives. That means everything—anchovies, cod liver oil, all of it. But most of us want to pick off toppings we don't like. No one promised that life would taste great all the time. But somehow God can turn even the most unpalatable situations into a gourmet feast.

WHEN IT COMES TO PROMISES, GOD DELIVERS!

We all stumble in many ways.

JAMES 3:2

Do not repay evil with evil or insult with
insult, but with blessing, because to this you
were called so that you may inherit a blessing.

1 PETER 3:9

You can't whitewash your sins and
get by with it; you find mercy
by admitting and leaving them.

PROVERBS 28:13 THE MESSAGE

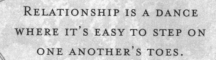

RELATIONSHIP IS A DANCE
WHERE IT'S EASY TO STEP ON
ONE ANOTHER'S TOES.

Blowing It

Paula ducked back out the restaurant door, her face flushed with anger. Before she had left school, she had asked her friend Jean to meet her for a milkshake that afternoon, but Jean had said she was too busy. Now here she was enjoying a sundae with a girl Paula had never met. Jean had lied to her!

In a split second, Paula reclassified Jean from friend to betrayer. How could she ever trust her again? Since she had lost her appetite, she went home without eating. When Jean spoke to her in the hall at school the next day, she just nodded without smiling and brushed on by.

Paula was still fuming inside when she overheard two classmates talking about how nice it was that Jean's cousin had dropped in from out of town for a visit. Paula's anger quickly turned to shame. "Lord, forgive me," she prayed.

Are you too quick to draw conclusions?

Give thanks in all circumstances.

1 THESSALONIANS 5:18

Then shalt thou have thy delight in the
Almighty, and shalt lift up thy face unto God.

JOB 22:26 KJV

Godliness with contentment is great gain.

1 TIMOTHY 6:6 NKJV

An Attitude of Gratitude

Cleaning toilets wasn't Dawn's idea of a great way to spend Friday night, but it was her bathroom, and she had promised her mom she'd keep it clean. As she began rinsing the sink, she caught sight of herself in the bathroom mirror—no makeup, her sweatshirt sleeves pushed up over her elbows, and a stray strand of hair escaping from her ponytail. *It's a good thing I'm not expecting company,* she thought.

Actually, that's what Dawn wanted most. She dreaded another weekend with no friends to talk to. Then it was almost as though she could hear God say, *How about talking to Me?*

"Okay, so what do we have to talk about?" she answered back.

Moments from her day came quickly to her mind—reasons for thanksgiving she'd almost overlooked. She even thanked God that she had a bathroom to clean, instead of an outhouse!

When you need someone to talk to, God is always there to keep you company.

> GOD CAN
> NO MORE DO
> WITHOUT US
> THAN WE CAN DO
> WITHOUT HIM.

I run in the path of your commands,
for you have set my heart free.

PSALM 119:32

If you use your lives to do the wrong things
your sinful selves want, you will die spiritually.
But if you use the Spirit's help to stop
doing the wrong things you do with
your body, you will have true life.

ROMANS 8:13 NCV

The Lord knows how to rescue the godly from
trial, and to keep the unrighteous under
punishment until the day of judgment.

2 PETER 2:9 RSV

The Road to Freedom

The flashing lights in Talia's rear-view mirror sent her heart into panic mode. She glanced at her speedometer. Reassured she was going the speed limit, she pulled over. The police car quickly darted past her in pursuit of some unknown emergency. Talia pulled back into traffic, breathing more easily.

She wondered how anyone could habitually break the speed limit. She knew she'd be a nervous wreck. She preferred following the rules and relaxing, instead of driving everywhere with one eye on the rear-view mirror, hoping she wouldn't get caught.

What about your relationship with Paul? The thought seemed to come from nowhere and pierced her heart. Her face flushed. Paul had wanted her to spend the night with him, and say she was staying over at a girl-friend's instead. And now she was on her way to his house. In that moment, she vowed not to compromise her values again. Looking in her rear-view mirror, Talia turned the car around.

Have you been compromising your values?

A GUILTY CONSCIENCE CAN BE A TICKET TO CHANGE.

Do your best, prepare for the worst—
then trust God to bring victory.

PROVERBS 21:31 THE MESSAGE

Be of good courage, and he shall strengthen
your heart, all ye that hope in the LORD.

PSALM 31:24 KJV

God has not given us a spirit of
fear and timidity, but of power,
love, and self-discipline.

2 TIMOTHY 1:7 NLT

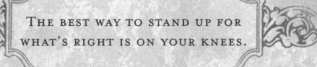

THE BEST WAY TO STAND UP FOR
WHAT'S RIGHT IS ON YOUR KNEES.

The Right Stuff

When it came to confrontation, Brooke's approach was like a wet noodle instead of an iron fist. Some people she confronted never even realized what she was doing. Quiet by nature, she was more comfortable not making waves. But she was trying to change and speak up when she needed to.

So when Brooke felt God prompt her to speak to her teacher about some major cheating in class going on behind his back, she prepared for their meeting on her knees. Being a whistleblower would make her unpopular, maybe even an outcast. She wasn't there to fix anything or name names; that was God's department. Outside her teacher's door, she took a deep breath and rapped on the door. When he indicated she should enter, she whispered a last, quick prayer before opening the door.

Where do you find the courage you need to do the right thing?

Love forgets mistakes.

PROVERBS 17:9 TLB

～

When you stand and pray, forgive
anything you may have against anyone,
so that your Father in heaven will
forgive the wrongs you have done.

MARK 11:25 TEV

～

If you forgive others their trespasses,
your heavenly Father will also forgive you.

MATTHEW 6:14 NRSV

～

Overlooked

As the pastor read off the Sunday school teachers' names, the volunteers rose to their feet to the sound of applause. But Terry remained in her seat, her eyes on her shoes and color rising in her cheeks. She'd taught the third-grade class for the last year, but for some reason, her name wasn't on the list. She knew it was just a mistake—a typing error—but it still hurt.

After the service, Terry decided to make a hasty retreat, but one of her students' mothers called out to her. The woman gave her a quick hug and said warmly, "I noticed they forgot to mention your name this morning. I just wanted to tell you how much your help in class has meant to Felicity. Thanks for everything." Right then Terry knew the oversight didn't matter.

Are you looking to someone for approval and recognition? Are you looking to God or people?

DON'T LET AN OFFENSE BUILD A RELATIONAL FENCE.

The desert shall rejoice,
and blossom as the rose.

ISAIAH 35:1 KJV

If you give, you will receive. Your gift will
return to you in full measure, pressed down,
shaken together to make room for more, and
running over. Whatever measure you use in
giving—large or small—it will be used to
measure what is given back to you.

LUKE 6:38 NLT

God is able to make all grace abound to you,
so that always having all sufficiency
in everything, you may have an
abundance for every good deed.

2 CORINTHIANS 9:8 NASB

Taken by Surprise

If someone asked Carmen what she wanted to do Friday night, babysitting three kids would have ranked down there with dusting the baseboards. After all, she'd had to contend with her own younger siblings all week. But her "regular" had asked—pleaded was more like it.

Carmen felt the Lord prompting her to say yes. So there she sat, making towers out of building blocks. The funny thing was, she had a really good time. The kids made her laugh and play, and they lavished her with love. Also, she later realized that the time spent with them gave her a new perspective on her own little brother and sister.

There are usually unexpected benefits to helping others. Why not let God surprise you?

GOD MAKES
EVERY DAY
AN ADVENTURE
INTO THE
UNEXPECTED.

Forgetting what is behind and straining
toward what is ahead, I press on toward
the goal to win the prize for which
God has called me heavenward.

PHILIPPIANS 3:13-14

Who pursued them, and passed safely by the
way that he had not gone with his feet?

ISAIAH 41:3 NKJV

Forget the former things; do not dwell
on the past. See, I am doing a new thing!
Now it springs up; do you not perceive it?

ISAIAH 43:18-19

YOU DON'T HAVE TO FORGET
SOMETHING TO LEAVE IT BEHIND.

Moving On

The beep of the microwave sounded, but Robbie hardly noticed. His attention was riveted to the familiar images in his hands. The focus of his attention wasn't anything new. Almost every morning since he had moved across country with his family, one of his numerous photo albums wound up in his hands. Some days, he could hardly gather the strength to put it away.

But this morning was different. Robbie had asked God to join him for a going-away party. He took one last look at the albums before storing them on the top shelf of his closet. It was time to make this new city his home—to make new friends and new memories. He'd lived in the old ones for too long. He said good-bye to each of the faces in the album and prayed God would help him take the first step toward whatever lay ahead.

God is good at drying our tears and putting a new song in our hearts.

Don't put your life in the hands of experts
who know nothing of life, of *salvation* life.

PSALM 146:3 THE MESSAGE

Evil men understand not judgment: but they
that seek the LORD understand all things.

PROVERBS 28:5 KJV

O Father, Lord of heaven and earth,
thank you for hiding the truth from those
who think themselves so wise and clever,
and for revealing it to the childlike.

MATTHEW 11:25 NLT

Bad Advice

It was some of the worst advice Jake had ever been given: "You have to try skydiving!" Hanging tight to the airplane seat, he now wished he hadn't said, "Why not?"

He contemplated other bad advice he'd listened to over the years. "Use the whole bottle of hot sauce; it'll taste better." "Hold this firecracker while I light it." And the worst, "You want to find God? Try these pills."

"Jake, your turn!" Wayne gestured as he yelled to his friend above the engine noise.

"Remind me never to listen to you again," Jake called back, before stepping out of the plane. He tensed up when he felt a sudden jerk, but then he realized it was just the chute opening. A moment later he was able to relax while floating slowly toward the ground far below. At that moment, Jake thanked God for the other sudden "jerk" that had pulled him out of drugs and back to Him.

DON'T LISTEN TO ADVICE THAT DOESN'T HAVE ITS FOUNDATION BOLTED TO GOD'S WORD.

Become friends with God;
he's already a friend with you.

2 CORINTHIANS 5:20 THE MESSAGE

For his own sake, the LORD won't
leave his people. Instead, he was
pleased to make you his own people.

1 SAMUEL 12:22 NCV

He heals the brokenhearted
and binds up their wounds.

PSALM 147:3

Last, Best Friend

Many of Pete's peers thought he was a nerd, and some of them didn't even know he existed. For the first sixteen years of his life, he spent a lot of time feeling sorry for himself because he had no friends. Just when he'd think he'd found someone he could talk to, his family would move. "I'm sorry, son. That's the life of a military family," his father would say.

Then, when he moved his junior year in high school, everything changed. First, he found a friend in Nick. Ironically, Nick moved away just a few weeks later, but not before he introduced Pete to his youth group. One Sunday night, during a youth group worship service, Pete found a permanent Friend: God.

From that day on, he knew he would always have Someone to talk to. He had found a Friend who wouldn't move.

Are you looking for a friend who will always be there for you? Turn to God, and you will find a forever Friend.

A FRIEND IS A PRESENT YOU GIVE YOURSELF.

I call as my heart grows faint; lead me
to the rock that is higher than I.

PSALM 61:2

In the day when I cried out, You answered me,
and made me bold with strength in my soul.

PSALM 138:3 NKJV

Cast not away therefore your confidence,
which hath great recompence of reward. For ye
have need of patience, that, after ye have done
the will of God, ye might receive the promise.

HEBREWS 10:35-36 KJV

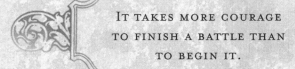

IT TAKES MORE COURAGE
TO FINISH A BATTLE THAN
TO BEGIN IT.

Climb Up

There are plenty of reasons to give up in life: fear, exhaustion, discouragement, complacency, pain, anger, impatience, and embarrassment, to name just a few. There are also those obstacles that just refuse to budge.

What have you given up on in life? It may be a project, a dream, or a relationship. It may even be hope or faith. What was your breaking point?

There will always be mountains that will rise beyond your endurance. There will be times when turning back seems like a wise thing to do. But the next time you're ready to give up, ask yourself a couple of questions: *Is this something I just don't want to face or can't face on my own? Am I giving up because I'm trying to accomplish this in my own strength instead of turning to God?* Then, pray and ask God to help you climb the mountain you are facing.

The LORD your God is with you. . . . He will
take great delight in you, he will quiet you with
his love, he will rejoice over you with singing.

ZEPHANIAH 3:17

You are precious in my sight,
and honored, and I love you.

ISAIAH 43:4 NRSV

God so loved the world that He gave
His only begotten Son, that whoever
believes in Him should not perish
but have everlasting life.

JOHN 3:16 NKJV

Letters of Love

Love letters come in all forms. Some are written in e-mails with e-card attachments. Some are covered with Xs and Os. Others are composed with such heartfelt emotion that they're read over and over until the paper has worn thin and the words are barely discernible. They touch the heart and warm the soul.

The Bible is God's love letter to the world. But even more importantly, it's a personal message to you. The words may remain the same for everyone, but God's relationship with you is different than His relationship with anyone else. How He communicates through those words, and what they will mean in relation to your life, will also differ. Cherish God's love letter to you, and read it over and over until you know the words by heart. It's more than a textbook or book of stories; and like a love letter, it's to be treasured.

> WHEN YOU READ GOD'S WORD, YOU MUST CONSTANTLY BE SAYING TO YOURSELF, "IT IS TALKING TO ME, AND ABOUT ME."

If you know the right thing to do and
don't do it, that, for you, is evil.

JAMES 4:17 THE MESSAGE

❧

In the past, people did not understand
God, and he ignored this. But now,
God tells all people in the world to
change their hearts and lives.

ACTS 17:30 NCV

❧

Sanctify the Lord God in your hearts, and
always be ready to give a defense to everyone
who asks you a reason for the hope that is
in you, with meekness and fear.

1 PETER 3:15 NKJV

❧

Break the Silence

Kyle sat on the edge of the deck, feet dangling and head down. He'd just received news that Jim had been arrested. He was told to soon expect a call from the police, inviting him for an interview. They'd grill him about what he knew of Jim's drug trafficking habits, and Kyle would walk away feeling just as rotten as he felt now.

Kyle wouldn't be indicted for what he knew. In fact, he had guessed wrong about what was going on. The clues led him to believe Jim was stealing from the cash register at work—he had so much money all of a sudden. Kyle mentally kicked himself for missing several opportunities to talk to him.

Once Jim had said something cryptic about "a secret that was making him a happy man." Then just last week he had said, "I could be in a lot of trouble soon." Now it might be too late to help him.

The only way to help others is to listen with your heart.

IF THE SILENCE IS DEAFENING, PERHAPS IT'S TIME TO BREAK IT.

Before you trust, you have to listen.
But unless Christ's Word is preached,
there's nothing to listen to.

ROMANS 10:17 THE MESSAGE

"Those who accept my commandments
and obey them are the ones who love me.
My Father will love those who love me; I too
will love them and reveal myself to them."

JOHN 14:21 TEV

We announce to you what we have seen
and heard, because we want you also to have
fellowship with us. Our fellowship is with
God the Father and with his Son, Jesus Christ.

1 JOHN 1:3 NCV

IF YOU CAN'T SEE THE TRUTH,
PERHAPS YOU SHOULD LISTEN
FOR IT INSTEAD.

A New Face

Ron was going to be here a while. "You'll make a full recovery," the doctor said, "but it will take some time." After three books, Ron was tired of reading. Instead, he decided to think.

On Thursday morning, his thoughts landed on the topic of religion. He'd studied them all—Buddhism, Islam, Christianity, and all sorts of New Age ideas; yet he still felt lost and alone. He tried to spend Friday in prayer, but he just didn't know to whom he should pray. *I just can't put a face on these religions,* he thought. Saturday, he was depressed.

Sunday brought a guest. "Hi, my name's Thom. I used to be a patient here. You need some company?" Ron wondered why a stranger wanted to spend time with him, and then it began to make sense. Thom was a Christian. His religion wasn't about rules or systems. It was about relationships. Suddenly, Christianity had a face—it looked like Thom.

This is what the LORD Almighty says:
"Give careful thought to your ways."

HAGGAI 1:5

———

When you are angry, do not sin, and be sure
to stop being angry before the end of the day.

EPHESIANS 4:26 NCV

———

Dear friends, never avenge yourselves.
Leave that to God. For it is written,
"I will take vengeance; I will repay
those who deserve it," says the Lord.

ROMANS 12:19 NLT

———

Reconsider

This is too easy, Terry thought, picking up a fat red water balloon from the bucket at his side. He grinned in anticipation as Vic walked toward him. Terry knew he would never see it coming.

This, Terry thought, aiming his throw, *is for those nasty things you said to me at school last week. Wait . . . not yet . . . make sure he's close enough . . . just a few more steps.* Just thinking about how Vic had made fun of him in the locker room made his blood boil. Finally, Terry could see Vic's eyes. He was—crying? *I wonder what that's all about? Vic's such a tough guy.* Terry gripped the water balloon tighter. *Why should I care? The guy's a total jerk!*

That's when the quiet voice of God asked, *Why should you care? Because I do.* Terry dropped the balloon. Maybe this wasn't such a good day for revenge after all.

ANGER IS NEVER
WITHOUT A
REASON, BUT
SELDOM WITH
A GOOD ONE.

The LORD preserves the faithful.

PSALM 31:23 NKJV

We do live in the world, but we do not fight
in the same way the world fights. We fight with
weapons that are different from those the
world uses. Our weapons have power from
God that can destroy the enemy's strong
places. We destroy people's arguments.

2 CORINTHIANS 10:3-4 NCV

Preach the word! Be ready in
season and out of season.

2 TIMOTHY 4:2 NKJV

Faith Target

Ostracized for speaking the truth about her faith, Gillian quickly became the target for troublemakers' taunts. Then the taunts turned violent. "Where's your God now?" an angry classmate mocked as he slammed her against the wall.

The bruises were still visible when she returned to school. Some kids who'd teased her before fell silent. No one had thought anyone would actually hurt her. Rumors spread quickly: "Jake tried to kill Gillian." "What did she do to deserve that?" "Nothing."

Gillian heard the whispers, too, and in time, the rumors—and the taunts—died down. In fact, she became something of a legend around the school halls. "I really admire you; you stand up for what you believe," students would say. Some even wanted to know how she did it. Gillian was happy to tell them about her God.

Are you willing to stand up for what you believe?

IT IS HUMAN TO STAND WITH THE CROWD. IT IS DIVINE TO STAND ALONE.

Be strong and of a good courage; be not afraid,
neither be thou dismayed: for the LORD thy
God is with thee whithersoever thou goest.

JOSHUA 1:9 KJV

The LORD is my light and my
salvation; Whom shall I fear?

PSALM 27:1 NKJV

Where God's love is, there is no fear,
because God's perfect love drives out fear.

1 JOHN 4:18 NCV

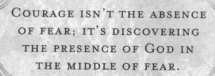

COURAGE ISN'T THE ABSENCE
OF FEAR; IT'S DISCOVERING
THE PRESENCE OF GOD IN
THE MIDDLE OF FEAR.

Gym Class

It was more terrifying than the deepest dungeon. It was more distasteful than a plateful of brussels sprouts. And it was listed on Jared's fall schedule: P.E. He knew it stood for "physical education," but he read it as "excruciating pain." It also stood for humiliation, because Jared's scrawny physique would stand in stark contrast to the muscular frames of the school jocks.

The first day they just sat and listened to the coach. There was no running and no showers, but Jared knew it wouldn't last. "Bring gym clothes tomorrow. We're playing basketball," the teacher said. *Not basketball!* Jared thought. *Anything but that!*

When Tuesday came, Jared prayed before he entered the boys' locker room. The door must have weighed a ton. He began to perspire. *I can't sweat! I'll have to take a shower! Well, Lord, looks like this is the semester I learn how to pray!*

The strangest things bring us to our knees, but God is always glad to hear from us.

Where there is no vision, the people perish.

PROVERBS 29:18 KJV

I cry out to God Most High, to God,
who fulfills his purpose for me.

PSALM 57:2

You are my rock and my protection.
For the good of your name, lead me
and guide me. . . . I give you my life.
Save me, LORD, God of truth.

PSALM 31:3-5 NCV

Beyond the Stars

"Don't you wish you could go there?" asked Kellie, who was lying in the grass next to her sister. A warm wind rustled their hair.

"To the stars?" Jessica asked. "I don't think so."

"But it's incredible. It's so vast. Don't you want to know if there's anybody but us out there?"

Jessica rolled over, rested her chin on her elbows, and asked, "Why do you always ask these impossible questions?"

"It helps put everything else in perspective," Kellie said. "It's good to think big thoughts."

"No," her sister replied, "it *hurts* to think big thoughts. I prefer to ride whatever wave comes my way."

Kellie looked over at her sister. "Don't you have any dreams, Jess? Any pictures in your head that keep you motivated to grow and learn?" It was a hard question. Secretly, Jessica longed to have big dreams. She longed to see further. *Father,* she prayed silently, *give me a dream too— one that will help other people.*

GOD PAINTS VISION INTO THE HEARTS OF THOSE WHO AREN'T AFRAID TO LOOK FURTHER THAN THEY CAN SEE.

My choice is you, GOD, first and only.
And now I find I'm *your* choice!

PSALM 16:5 THE MESSAGE

～

You who seek God, may your hearts live!

PSALM 69:32

～

"I have not come to invite good people but
sinners to change their hearts and lives."

LUKE 5:32 NCV

～

What Is That Loud Buzzing?

The day began with a buzzing alarm, a slap of the hand onto the snooze button, another buzzing, another slapping, another buzzing, and finally, a slow crawl out of bed. Before Tricia had invited her to church, Erica had always enjoyed sleeping in on Sunday mornings. No more.

But Tricia was a good friend, and there *was* something about this church that seemed to call to her almost as loudly as the alarm buzzer. Sometimes during the message, Erica would get a little sleepy—but not this morning. The pastor seemed to be talking directly to her. When he invited anyone looking for God to see him after the service, she was first in line.

Do you have a friend who needs to hear about the love of God? Do you have a friend who is hurting and could use some encouragement? Be a *real* friend; invite him or her to church.

IT'S INCREDIBLY EXCITING TO CHOOSE TO FOLLOW GOD AND INFINITELY HUMBLING TO REALIZE GOD CHOSE YOU.

Whatever I have, wherever I am,
I can make it through anything in
the One who makes me who I am.

PHILIPPIANS 4:13 THE MESSAGE

Enter his gates with thanksgiving;
go into his courts with praise.
Give thanks to him and bless his name.

PSALM 100:4 NLT

The LORD is my shepherd;
I have everything I need.

PSALM 23:1 NLT

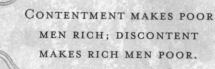

CONTENTMENT MAKES POOR
MEN RICH; DISCONTENT
MAKES RICH MEN POOR.

Modest Circumstance

The tiny stove only had two working burners—
enough for spaghetti and sauce or hot dogs and
beans. Melody wasn't sure which meal Carmen's
mother would be serving tonight, but it didn't matter.
She made each one with equal enthusiasm. As Melody
knocked on the apartment door, she wondered how *she*
would survive in a two-room, rundown apartment.

"Come on in. Mom's made you a special dinner
tonight." That meant spaghetti. Though she often felt
guilty for having so much when Carmen had nearly
nothing, Melody still loved visiting her because she
was always so thankful. "Thank you, God, for blessing
my life so richly," Carmen prayed, as always. Today,
they'd talk about gardens, even though Carmen's
apartment was on the seventh floor.

Melody had a lot to learn. Her friend knew everything there was to know about gardens. But more than
that, she knew about contentment. Perhaps that's why
Melody kept coming to visit.

How contented are you?

Learn the unforced rhythms of grace.
I won't lay anything heavy or ill-fitting
on you. Keep company with me and
you'll learn to live freely and lightly.

MATTHEW 11:29-30 THE MESSAGE

We are hard-pressed on every side, yet
not crushed; we are perplexed, but not
in despair; persecuted, but not forsaken;
struck down, but not destroyed.

2 CORINTHIANS 4:8-9 NKJV

I find rest in God; only he gives me hope.

PSALM 62:5 NCV

Not Too Heavy

Belinda was disillusioned soon after she'd become a Christian. "Your life will never be the same," her friends had told her. But her problems remained.

"So what's supposed to be different?" she asked Darcy one day.

"Well, we still have problems. One difference is that we have Someone to share them with," her friend said.

Belinda's frustration turned to curiosity. "You mean God?"

"Yes," Darcy answered.

"Is He going to pass my exams for me too? Is He going to work out the problems with my mom?"

Carefully and thoughtfully, Darcy explained God's promise to always be near and His promise of rest for weary souls. Then she added, "You've been flying solo for a long time, Belinda. Just hang in there with God, and let Him sit in the pilot's seat for a change."

When God comes into our lives, our problems don't just disappear. But we do receive a new perspective. God *can* lead you to solutions. The problems seem more manageable with the Creator of the universe by your side.

THE GREATER THE DIFFICULTY, THE MORE GLORY IN SURMOUNTING IT. SKILLFUL PILOTS GAIN THEIR REPUTATION FROM STORMS AND TEMPESTS.

"Put your mind on your life with God.
The way to life—to God!—is vigorous and
requires your total attention."

LUKE 13:24 THE MESSAGE

≈

The fruit of the righteous is a tree of
life, and he who wins souls is wise.

PROVERBS 11:30 NKJV

≈

You shall receive power when the Holy Spirit
has come upon you; and you shall be my
witnesses in Jerusalem and in all Judea
and Sama'ria and to the end of the earth.

ACTS 1:8 RSV

≈

Role Reversal

Stephanie idolized her big sister, Sherrie. Sherrie was a straight-A student, scholarship magnet, and beauty queen. She was good at everything. Sherrie was Stephanie's inspiration.

But when Sherrie went away to college, she pretty much gave up on God. "Don't have much time for that anymore, Steph," she said, during a rare Internet chat. Stephanie loved her big sister, but putting a relationship with God in the "if I have time" box didn't sit well with her.

Many years later, while visiting her younger sibling, Sherrie said, "I've messed up a ton in my life, but I want you to know I'm changing all that. In fact, I want to thank you."

"Thank me?" Stephanie said. "For what?"

"In college I looked up to you, Sis. You took your relationship with God seriously. I didn't—and I paid the price. But you never gave up on me, and now I'm back." It was a glimpse of God's love in both their lives.

GOOD EXAMPLE HAS TWICE THE VALUE OF GOOD ADVICE.

Cast your cares on the LORD
and he will sustain you.

PSALM 55:22

Cast all your anxiety on him
because he cares for you.

1 PETER 5:7

In the multitude of my anxieties within me,
Your comforts delight my soul.

PSALM 94:19 NKJV

CASTING OFF WHAT YOU DON'T
NEED MAKES IT EASIER TO
HOLD ONTO WHAT YOU DO.

Let It Fly

Horseshoes wasn't a game Rory had ever longed to play. But when Granddad suggested he give it a go, he figured if he declined, cribbage would be next on the agenda. His grandfather began by putting several horseshoes in Rory's hand. "Weighty little buggers, aren't they?" Granddad said with a wink.

Rory watched his grandfather carefully pitch several horseshoes at the metal pin in the ground. Every shot made a satisfying "clank" as it reached its destination. His own attempts, however, showed considerably less success. Getting discouraged, he asked his grandfather why he enjoyed this game so much.

"I'll tell you why," Granddad said, with a sudden air of seriousness. "Every time I throw one of them horseshoes, I picture myself casting one of my problems on the Lord. By the time the game's finished, I always feel a lot better!"

Sometimes, casting your cares on the Lord works more like a boomerang than a horseshoe. The key is in the release.

Nothing is secret that will not be
revealed, nor *anything* hidden that
will not be known and come to light.

LUKE 8:17 NKJV

☰

You have set our iniquities before you,
our secret sins in the light of your presence.

PSALM 90:8

☰

We have renounced the hidden things
of shame, not walking in craftiness nor
handling the word of God deceitfully,
but by manifestation of the truth
commending ourselves to every man's
conscience in the sight of God.

2 CORINTHIANS 4:2 NKJV

☰

Undercover Operation

Mark heard his mom's scream over the sound of the shower. He threw a towel around himself and hurried downstairs. What he didn't expect to find was his mother doubled over with laughter.

"Mom! You scared me," Mark said, annoyed. "What happened?" His mother, with tears of laughter, pointed to the crawlspace doorway. There was the sack of potatoes Mark had tossed in a couple of months ago and had promptly forgotten. In the damp darkness, the potatoes had happily sprouted, wildly sending shoots in every direction, blocking the entire doorway.

Some things grow best in the dark. Secrets, for instance. Is there anything in your life you don't want others to know? Perhaps it is a habit or addiction. Your Internet surfing? Your past? Bringing secrets to light can be painful, but keeping them in the dark only allows them to grow. You can trust the light of God's love to help you clean out the crawlspace of your heart.

> NOTHING
> IS
> SO BURDENSOME
> AS
> A SECRET.

Keep company with GOD, get in on the best.

PSALM 37:4 THE MESSAGE

God keeps his word even when the
whole world is lying through its teeth.

ROMANS 3:4 THE MESSAGE

All Scripture is given by God and is useful
for teaching, for showing people what is
wrong in their lives, for correcting faults,
and for teaching how to live right.

2 TIMOTHY 3:16 NCV

Undeserved Abundance

The woman in the tollbooth refused Simon's outstretched dollar bill. "The man in the car ahead of you paid your toll, sir," she explained. Confused, Simon stumbled over a word of thanks and quickly drove off in search of the car that proceeded him. When he finally caught up with the white sedan, he glanced at the elderly driver, but he did not know him.

Simon motioned to the mysterious benefactor to roll down his window. "Why'd you pay for me?" he yelled across the lane.

The man just waved, yelled a friendly, "Have a good day," and disappeared into the traffic. Simon was baffled. *Something for nothing— God's the only One who does stuff like that,* he thought. But he felt good, unexpectedly blessed. That's when he decided that on the way home, he'd surprise whoever was behind him by paying his or her toll.

Blessings are undeserved, yet God showers you with them every day. How can you pass the joy on to others?

BE KIND: EVERYONE YOU MEET IS FIGHTING A HARD BATTLE.

Open up before GOD, keep nothing back;
he'll do whatever needs to be done.

PSALM 37:5 THE MESSAGE

He can help those who are tempted, because
he himself suffered and was tempted.

HEBREWS 2:18 NCV

Submit to God. Resist the devil
and he will flee from you.

JAMES 4:7 NKJV

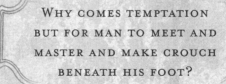

WHY COMES TEMPTATION
BUT FOR MAN TO MEET AND
MASTER AND MAKE CROUCH
BENEATH HIS FOOT?

Breaking Rusted Locks

Dennis wedged the crowbar between the lock and the latch on the cabinet. *Snap!* The latch broke off with such force that he fell backward and stumbled into a pyramid of paint cans.

"Well, I deserved that," he said to himself. He opened the cabinet. Stacks of pornographic magazines filled the two shelves. After a brief pause, he began tossing the magazines into a big trash bin. "Okay, God," he prayed, "You know my darkest secrets. Now please help me to find the light again."

With the shelves empty, Dennis wheeled the bin to the back yard and dumped its contents onto the already burning fire. When the fire died down, he returned to the basement. He picked up the latch with the lock still attached and targeted the trashcan. But then he stopped. Instead, he took the lock to his bedroom and set it on his desk. It remains there as a reminder to keep nothing from God. And it's working.

The LORD is close to the brokenhearted.

PSALM 34:18

He comforts us every time we have trouble,
so when others have trouble, we can comfort
them with the same comfort God gives us.

2 CORINTHIANS 1:4 NCV

Do not be afraid, nor be dismayed, for the
LORD your God is with you wherever you go.

JOSHUA 1:9 NKJV

Shattered

The plate slipped from Debbie's hands and shattered on the tile floor. She stood there for a moment, stunned. Then the tears began to flow. The plate had been her mother's, one of the only reminders Debbie had of her. Now it was gone, broken beyond repair. The fine china was nothing but flowered shards scattered beneath her feet.

And nothing could put Humpty-Dumpty together again, she thought. As the nursery rhyme ran through her head, her heart wrote an alternate ending. *Except God,* it assured her. Looking at that plate reminded her of how she'd felt when her mother died—broken, useless. But God had put her back together. Even though the plate was gone, Debbie's memories were intact. Better yet, so was her heart.

A broken heart can be a consequence of life, but that doesn't mean you should try to get accustomed to the pain. Not only is God close to the brokenhearted, He also heals them.

GOD DOESN'T MAKE BROKEN HEARTS AS GOOD AS NEW—HE MAKES THEM NEW.

God, a most fierce warrior, is at my side.

JEREMIAH 20:11 THE MESSAGE

Who is this King of glory? The LORD strong
and mighty, the LORD mighty in battle.

PSALM 24:8

God himself shall be with them,
and be their God.

REVELATION 21:3 KJV

Inhale the Breath of God

Becoming a Christian had been a relatively easy decision for Jon. Though he felt no overwhelming change or any other emotional charge, he knew he'd joined God's family. Gaining wisdom and knowledge had always been important quests for him, so he was anxious to quickly learn all he could about God's wisdom.

"Lord, make me wise," he prayed. He dove into Bible study, reading every passage about wisdom he could find. He wanted to know everything there was to know about wisdom—and he wanted it now. But Jon didn't sense any greater ability to reason, any hint of added discernment. In fact, it seemed God was silent. Weeks passed, and he felt no wiser.

Then, one day he said in frustration, "God, I don't understand You—or anything much about this life." And that very day, Jon began to grow in wisdom.

KNOWLEDGE IS PROUD THAT HE HAS LEARNED SO MUCH; WISDOM IS HUMBLE THAT HE KNOWS NO MORE.

Seek peace and pursue it.

PSALM 34:14

⟡

He that will love life, and see good days . . .
let him seek peace, and ensue it.

1 PETER 3:10-11 KJV

⟡

Strive for perfection; listen to my appeals;
agree with one another; live in peace. And the
God of love and peace will be with you.

2 CORINTHIANS 13:11 TEV

⟡

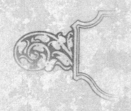

PEACE IS LIBERTY
IN TRANQUILITY.

A Peaceful Pursuit

"Peace on earth, goodwill toward men" isn't just a sentiment on a Christmas card. It was initially a greeting straight from heaven. Having God's peace in your heart is one thing. But what does peace on earth look like? Is it just a platitude, or do you think it can take place in your daily life? Is it something God will bring about, or are you part of the solution?

Peace is often pictured as a quiet, pastoral scene, almost devoid of movement. But peace can be found in the laughter of friends as easily as in solitude and meditation.

Sometimes making peace takes work; it has to be pursued. If there is a conflict in a relationship, you may have to confront a person in love in order to find peace again. Ask God for help as you strive to pursue and maintain peace in all of your relationships; and most importantly, ask Him to fill your life with His peace.

Who despises the day of small things?

ZECHARIAH 4:10

You are of God, little children, and have
overcome them, because He who is in you
is greater than he who is in the world.

1 JOHN 4:4 NKJV

Are not two sparrows sold for a farthing?
and one of them shall not fall on the ground
without your Father. But the very hairs of your
head are all numbered. Fear ye not therefore,
ye are of more value than many sparrows.

MATTHEW 10:29-31 KJV

Not Insignificant

Zack had tinkered with the computer for three hours, trying without success to find out why it wouldn't boot up. He had replaced the video card, the CPU, the power supply, and even the sound card, but nothing seemed to work. He dreaded the thought of taking the beast to the repair shop—that computer was his life.

As he was about to give up, he noticed a tiny wire hanging free inside the case. Upon careful inspection, he determined it connected the case's power button to the motherboard. Sure enough, once the tiny wire was plugged in, the computer started up without a hitch.

Little things are not always insignificant. Like the wire in the computer case, often they can provide the solution to a problem—and turn a good day into a great one.

SOMETIMES THE SMALLEST THINGS CAN HAVE THE GREATEST POWER.

By using Scripture, [God's people] can be
completely prepared to do every good thing.

2 TIMOTHY 3:17 NIRV

The word of God is living and active.
Sharper than any double-edged sword,
it penetrates even to dividing soul and
spirit, joints and marrow; it judges the
thoughts and attitudes of the heart.

HEBREWS 4:12

Heaven and earth will disappear,
but my words will remain forever.

MARK 13:31 NLT

Scripture Surfing

The premium cable package was finally at Greg's fingertips. He sat down with the remote control, ready for action. He could choose between sports, movies, news, weather, music videos, animals or history. He could even travel to exciting places—all without ever getting off the sofa. He was overwhelmed with the options.

That's how Greg felt about the Bible too. He never knew if he should start at the beginning, follow a Bible study book, or open it randomly and pick out a "verse for the day." He knew the Bible contained everything he needed to face life: information on relationships, guidelines for money management, what to do about temptation, lists of things to do and not to do. Yet, once again, he was overwhelmed with all the options.

Remember, the Bible isn't a crash course in life; it's a conversation with the living God. If you're unsure where to start, seek out some guidance, and then plunge in.

BE ASTONISHED THAT GOD SHOULD HAVE WRITTEN TO US.

I will remove from them their heart of
stone and give them a heart of flesh.

EZEKIEL 11:19

We have around us many people whose lives
tell us what faith means. So let us run the
race that is before us and never give up.

HEBREWS 12:1 NCV

You are the light of the world. A city that is
set on a hill cannot be hidden. Nor do they
light a lamp and put it under a basket, but
on a lampstand, and it gives light to all who
are in the house. Let your light so shine
before men, that they may see your good
works and glorify your Father in heaven.

MATTHEW 5:14-16 NKJV

A THOUSAND WORDS WILL
NOT LEAVE AS DEEP AN
IMPRESSION AS ONE DEED.

A Gentle Tap

Three years—that's how long Bob had prayed for Joe to explore a relationship with God. Bob hadn't been obnoxious. In fact, it wasn't until three months into their friendship that he even mentioned he went to church.

Joe simply said, "Good for you."

In time, they came to a mutual understanding about their beliefs. Each said: "I'm not going to hide what I believe, but I won't force my beliefs down your throat." Perhaps because of this honest approach, they developed a strong bond. When Bob got sick, Joe covered for him at work. When Joe's dad died, Bob was there for him.

One day, however, Bob saw the first crack in Joe's heart. "This God of yours is tapping on my heart," he said. Bob couldn't restrain his broad smile.

Do your actions draw others to God?

The righteous will live by faith.

ROMANS 1:17

There is a way that seems right to a man,
But its end is the way of death.

PROVERBS 14:12 NKJV

We live by what we believe,
not by what we can see.

2 CORINTHIANS 5:7 NCV

Faith Walk

"**I** won't follow a God I can't understand," was Jason's standard reply to anyone who tried to talk to him about spiritual things. "Why is there suffering? How could God create the world out of nothing? Why would Someone that powerful care about me anyway?"

Kurt knew Jason's questions were valid, but his reasoning was faulty. "Do you really understand how a heavy airplane flies through the air?" he asked him. Jason had to admit he didn't. "But you still fly in one," Kurt continued. "You don't understand the chemistry behind cold medicine, but you take it when you need it. You admit you don't know how life began, but that doesn't stop you from taking your next breath. That's what faith's all about."

No, we can't see or understand God, but we can see and feel signs of His love for us everywhere. And He's our Maker, our Heavenly Father—that's why He cares.

> ONLY TO
> OUR INTELLECT
> IS GOD
> INCOMPREHENSIBLE;
> NOT TO
> OUR LOVE.

I do not understand my own actions.
For I do not do what I want, but
I do the very thing I hate.

ROMANS 7:15 RSV

A man shall eat good by
the fruit of his mouth.

PROVERBS 13:2 KJV

Words kill, words give life; they're either
poison or fruit—you choose.

PROVERBS 18:21 THE MESSAGE

Look Next Time

"**D**river's license and registration," the policeman ordered, "out of the wallet." As Paul reached into his wallet, he wondered if all officers had such eloquent speaking ability. Of course, he wasn't one to talk. His mouth had gotten him into trouble more times than he could count.

Paul wasn't a mean-spirited person. Most of the time, people loved being around him for his dry wit. But once in a while, his wit would take the form of a dragon and scorch all in its path. He never intended to hurt anyone, but the fallout was often devastating. It even cost him his girlfriend.

There were days when Paul felt all he did was apologize. "I'm sorry, Officer," he said, snapping back to the moment. "I didn't see that car when I was backing up."

Tearing off the ticket, the officer spoke three words, "Look next time."

Paul knew instantly this was wise advice for all of life, and he said, "I will."

WORDS
ARE
LOADED
PISTOLS.

He has showed you, O man, what is good.
And what does the LORD require of you?
To act justly and to love mercy and to
walk humbly with your God.

MICAH 6:8

I know also, my God, that You test the heart
and have pleasure in uprightness.

1 CHRONICLES 29:17 NKJV

O LORD, who may abide in your tent?
Who may dwell on your holy hill? Those
who walk blamelessly, and do what is right,
and speak the truth from their heart.

PSALM 15:1-2 NRSV

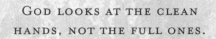

GOD LOOKS AT THE CLEAN
HANDS, NOT THE FULL ONES.

Questions of Conscience

The cashier handed Tricia her change. With a quick thank you, she headed out the door, putting the cash in her wallet. *But how could there be a ten?* she wondered. She'd just paid for the earrings with the only bill she had—a ten. She realized the cashier must have mistakenly thought she'd paid with a twenty. She turned to go back when something inside her asked, *Why? You sure could use the extra cash.*

Tricia knew her mom or dad would return it. They'd feel that's what God wanted them to do because it was the right thing. But she wasn't so sure about all this God stuff. If God wasn't real, why did walking out with this money feel so wrong? She walked back inside to return the money.

God has built into us an inner moral voice—our conscience. Listen to what that voice is saying to you; then act accordingly. This is the way to establish inner peace.

When anxiety was great within me, your
consolation brought joy to my soul.

PSALM 94:19

We have troubles all around us, but we are
not defeated. We do not know what to do, but
we do not give up the hope of living. We are
persecuted, but God does not leave us. We are
hurt sometimes, but we are not destroyed.

2 CORINTHIANS 4:8-9 NCV

If thou seest the oppression of the poor,
and violent perverting of judgment and
justice in a province, marvel not at the
matter: for he that is higher than the highest
regardeth; and there be higher than they.

ECCLESIASTES 5:8 KJV

God's Echo

The cliff's edge seemed the perfect place to sit and contemplate the news. "I feel as far from you right now, God, as this edge of the cliff is from the other side," Rachel said as she stared across the chasm.

Any other day, she'd have been overwhelmed by the beauty of the sunset and the meandering river far below. But not today. Rachel, instead, was overwhelmed by this world: injustice in Africa, a killer earthquake in India, and—betrayal by her best friend. "Where are you, God?" she called out across the canyon. Her voice echoed a few seconds, then died away. She began to cry. Then, she sensed a faint sound returning to her, and she knew that she was not alone; God was in those echoes.

Human beings often fail us, but God never will. That doesn't make the betrayal of a friend less painful, but it does give us Someone dependable to go to for comfort.

PROVIDENCE HAS AT ALL TIMES BEEN MY ONLY DEPENDENCE, FOR ALL OTHER RESOURCES SEEM TO HAVE FAILED US.

Do not be far from me, for trouble
is near and there is no one to help.

PSALM 22:11

❦

The ways of God are without fault. The Lord's
words are pure. He is a shield to those who
trust him. Who is God? Only the Lord.
Who is the Rock? Only our God. God is my
protection. He makes my way free from fault.

PSALM 18:30-32 NCV

❦

"The mountains may depart and the hills
disappear, but even then I will remain
loyal to you. My covenant of blessing
will never be broken," says the
LORD, who has mercy on you.

ISAIAH 54:10 NLT

❦

Temperamental Truth

Yolanda felt she'd been on an emotional roller coaster for the last week. That was to be expected with everything she was going through. But what she didn't expect was to feel so far away from God. Especially, because she'd felt so close to Him just yesterday. Where had He gone? She got on her knees for the third time that day. Even if she couldn't feel God, she knew He was the only One she could turn to right now; so she continued to reach out, even when she felt there was no one reaching back.

Feeling the intimacy of God's presence is a wonderful thing. But on this earth, it's most likely a fleeting experience, not a perpetual state. How you feel about something isn't an accurate gauge of what's really true. When your emotions say that God is far away, remind yourself of what is true—that God is always with you, and that nothing can separate us from His love.

> WE NEED NEVER SHOUT ACROSS THE SPACES TO AN ABSENT GOD. HE IS NEARER THAN OUR OWN SOUL, CLOSER THAN OUR MOST SECRET THOUGHTS.

If you do not stand firm in your faith,
you will not stand at all.

ISAIAH 7:9

The wise people will shine like the brightness
of the sky. Those who teach others to live
right will shine like stars forever and ever.

DANIEL 12:3 NCV

How can people call for help if they
don't know who to trust? And how can
they know who to trust if they haven't
heard of the One who can be trusted?
And how can they hear if nobody tells them?

ROMANS 10:14 THE MESSAGE

TRUTH IS INCONTROVERTIBLE.
PANIC MAY RESENT IT; IGNORANCE
MAY DERIDE IT; MALICE MAY
DISTORT IT; *BUT THERE IT IS.*

War of Words

"Anyone who believes in a God who communicates on a personal level with us mere mortals has got to be an idiot," Hal announced authoritatively. Those who were gathered around the lunch table didn't say a word. Everyone at school knew that Hal wasn't one to take opposition lightly.

On the outside, Eric peacefully munched on a bag of potato chips; but inside, he felt a war erupting. Hal's words went against everything he believed to be true, but he didn't know what to do. Should he speak up, engage Hal in a conversation, or just hold his tongue and add him to his prayer list?

Sometimes the "Hals" of the world want nothing more than to hear that what they believe is untrue—that they really can know a personal God who cares for them individually. Don't be afraid to speak what is true; you may just be surprised at the result.

He answered their prayers,
because they trusted in him.

1 CHRONICLES 5:20

Call to Me, and I will answer you,
and show you great and mighty
things, which you do not know.

JEREMIAH 33:3 NKJV

Therefore I say to you, all things for which
you pray and ask, believe that you have
received them, and they shall be granted you.

MARK 11:24 NASB

Prayer Protocol

Ordering pizza by phone was enough to prompt Jackie to pray. She had a hard time communicating, especially with strangers. Most of them tried to be polite, but her stuttering made the most casual conversation waver between uncomfortable and impossible.

But when Jackie prayed, she knew God wasn't in a hurry for her to finish a sentence. He had all the time in the world. That's one reason she often prayed aloud; to remind herself that even when the words she was trying to say weren't coming across perfectly, God understood. He loved her just the same.

How you sound when you pray doesn't matter to God. You may have the vocabulary of an evangelist or a child. You may pray confidently in front of a group or never have spoken a prayer aloud in your life. It's all the same to His ears, for He hears your heart.

PRAYER REQUIRES MORE OF THE HEART THAN OF THE TONGUE.

Without having seen him you love him;
though you do not now see him you
believe in him and rejoice with
unutterable and exalted joy.

1 PETER 1:8 RSV

These are written that you may believe that
Jesus is the Christ, the Son of God, and that
by believing you may have life in his name.

JOHN 20:31

Blessed are those who have not
seen and yet have believed.

JOHN 20:29

Waiting for the Rain

In the dark cavern of an office where Michael worked after school, there was just one small window. It sat just above the green lawn outside the front of the office building.

Michael sat alone with the innards of a half-dozen computers strewn across his worktable. He heard nothing but the hum of hard drives and spinning disks, and the occasional beep. As his tired eyes looked out the window, he noticed rain had begun to fall. He sighed. After cramming for finals all week, it was all he could do to stay awake at work.

Michael paused for a few moments and asked God for a refreshing rain in his life. Then, he got out of his chair, climbed the stairs, and walked outside. He stood in the rain, arms held wide, face to the sky, enjoying the blessings he knew would come soon enough.

Ask God for the refreshing rain of His love in your life.

THE QUALITY OF MERCY IS NOT STRAIN'D, IT DROPPETH AS THE GENTLE RAIN FROM HEAVEN.

I know, my God, that you test the heart and
are pleased with integrity. All these things
have I given willingly and with honest intent.

1 CHRONICLES 29:17

I have done what is fair and right.
Don't leave me to those who wrong me.

PSALM 119:121 NCV

To do what is right and just is more
acceptable to the LORD than sacrifice.

PROVERBS 21:3

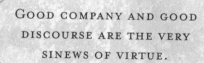

GOOD COMPANY AND GOOD
DISCOURSE ARE THE VERY
SINEWS OF VIRTUE.

Under the Influence

Has a red shirt ever ended up in your washing machine with a load of whites? What happens? Pink socks for everyone. The red shirt may not seem to fade much, but it sure leaves its mark on everything around it.

The same thing happens when you spend a lot of time with people who do things that go against God's law of love. You begin to pick up their "hue." Consider using God's name as a curse, for instance. This may not be a habit you've struggled with, but after spending time with people to whom it's second nature, you may not notice it much anymore. It may even seem humorous, at times. The next thing you know, words you never thought you'd say are slipping out of your mouth.

This doesn't mean you should never spend time with people whose values differ from God's. You can't love people without spending time with them. But if their habits begin influencing your own, watch out. You soon may find yourself in hot water.

"Love the Lord your God with all
your heart and with all your
soul and with all your mind."

MATTHEW 22:37

God wants you to be holy and to
stay away from sexual sins. He wants
each of you to learn to control your own
body in a way that is holy and honorable.
Don't use your body for sexual sin like
the people who do not know God.

1 THESSALONIANS 4:3-5 NCV

Clothe yourselves with the Lord Jesus Christ
and forget about satisfying your sinful self.

ROMANS 13:14 NCV

Stray Thoughts

It all began with a thought—harmless enough. But that thought led to another, which became a second look. That second look progressed to a minor indiscretion, which gave birth to a lie and led to rationalization. Before Michael knew it, he was having sex with a girl from the fast-food restaurant where he worked nights and weekends. His friends wondered how Mr. Righteous could have gotten involved in something like this.

Turning away from God is like setting up a line of dominoes: a little dishonesty here, a white lie there, a secret habit off in the corner somewhere. One by one, each domino is placed right behind the other. All it takes is a little added pressure for the whole line to come tumbling down.

Other people can't see your every thought, but God knows them intimately. And if it all begins with a thought, it can end there as well. Willpower is useless. (Try *not* thinking of a pink elephant!) God's power is the only answer.

WHAT WE THINK ABOUT WHEN WE ARE FREE TO THINK ABOUT WHAT WE WILL— THAT IS WHAT WE ARE OR WILL SOON BECOME.

There is no fear in love, but
perfect love casts out fear.

1 JOHN 4:18 RSV

Nothing bad will happen to you;
no disaster will come to your home.
He has put his angels in charge of
you to watch over you wherever you go.

PSALM 91:10-11 NCV

In him I trust, and I will not be afraid.
What can a mere human being do to me?

PSALM 56:11 TEV

No Fear

As a twelve-year-old, Dayna used to lie awake listening to the sounds of the night. When her parents hosted visitors for the evening, she would strain to hear their conversations and fall asleep easily to the familiar rhythm of voices. But when there were no voices, she could not sleep. The foreign creaks and groans that littered the night opened her eyes wide in fear. Even the somewhat familiar sound of the furnace seemed suddenly menacing in the dark.

Dayna prayed during those nights—that she might fall asleep, and that the sounds would go away. In those prayers, she pictured a loving God—a God who would not want her to feel afraid. As a twelve-year-old, Dayna learned a lot about life. She learned that fear was a real thing. But mostly she learned that God's love was bigger than fear.

Don't let fear rob you of your peace. Entrust yourself to God.

> GOD INCARNATE IS THE END OF FEAR; AND THE HEART THAT REALIZES THAT HE IS IN THE MIDST . . . WILL BE QUIET IN THE MIDST OF ALARM.

"Why do you look at the speck of sawdust
in your brother's eye and pay no attention
to the plank in your own eye?"

MATTHEW 7:3

If I speak in the tongues of men and of
angels, but have not love, I am only a
resounding gong or a clanging cymbal.

1 CORINTHIANS 13:1

These three things continue forever: faith,
hope, and love. And the greatest of these is love.

1 CORINTHIANS 13:13 NCV

FAITHFULNESS IN LITTLE
THINGS IS A BIG THING.

Difficult Things

The sound of rain pounding on metal threatened to drown out Greg's thoughts as he sat in the idling car. He watched as a cardboard "GARAGE SALE" sign raced down the river that had formed just outside the driver's side door. "I'll get soaked," he reasoned. Straining to look through the fogging passenger window, he noticed a light on in the small house. "They don't know I'm coming . . . what if they. . . ."

Then Greg remembered why he was there. He'd become a volunteer for a community outreach program. He'd thought he'd be painting houses or mowing lawns; but instead, he was bringing a pizza to strangers.

"Dear God, help me to do this right," he prayed. He stepped out of the car into ice-cold, ankle-deep water and smack dab into a glimpse of an invisible God.

Don't let fear or uneasiness keep you from reaching out to others. The rewards go both ways.

Some trust in chariots and some
in horses, but we trust in the
name of the LORD our God.

PSALM 20:7

≋

Let us hold on firmly to the hope we profess,
because we can trust God to keep his promise.

HEBREWS 10:23 TEV

≋

As for God, His way is perfect;
The word of the LORD is proven;
He is a shield to all who trust in Him.

2 SAMUEL 22:31 NKJV

≋

What Do You Really Know?

Greg was the most obnoxious person you could ever know. He was a know-it-all who knew a lot. In a conversation about evolution, he would readily quote at least two dozen fact-based studies in support of his opinion. His knowledge of sports kept him spouting statistics for hours. But if you wanted a real lecture, all you had to do was mention God. He knew everything there was to know about God. He had read through the Bible five times and kept his bookshelves stocked with commentaries and theology books.

But the other day, Greg discovered something he didn't know. He didn't find it in a book. Instead, he found it after pondering the words of his six-year-old niece. She said, "How can someone with such big words have such a small heart?" Head knowledge and long-winded talk pale in comparison to a sincere and loving heart.

THOSE WHO WOULD KNOW MUCH AND LOVE LITTLE, WILL REMAIN EVER AT THE BEGINNING OF A GODLY LIFE.

Find a quiet, secluded place so you won't be tempted to role-play before God. Just be there as simply and honestly as you can manage. The focus will shift from you to God, and you will begin to sense his grace.

MATTHEW 6:6 THE MESSAGE

Pride leads to disgrace, but with humility comes wisdom.

PROVERBS 11:2 NLT

Whoever exalts himself will be humbled, and he who humbles himself will be exalted.

MATTHEW 23:12 NKJV

The Garden Shed

Cate knew the spotlight like an old friend. Most of the time, she sang at church, and she was good. Each performance ended with generous applause. The first few Sundays, she'd felt humbled by the response. Then she began to feel pretty good about her contribution to the church services—too good. She became proud.

Cate's close friend Debby put an end to that one Sunday when she said, "The service isn't about *you*, Cate. It's about God." And that's when Cate rediscovered her mother's garden shed. In that dirty, dusty, musty room she met God. There was no audience to sing to, no dramatic musical score, only the watchful spider and the erratic buzzing of flies.

The garden shed changed her Sunday morning voice. And people noticed. People no longer said, "You're great!" Now they said, "God really spoke to me through your song." Thanks to an honest friend and a garden shed, the Creator of Cate's talent was getting the applause.

THERE IS BUT A STEP BETWEEN A PROUD MAN'S GLORY AND HIS DISGRACE.

The Lord is near.

PHILIPPIANS 4:5

Indeed our fellowship is with the Father,
and with His Son Jesus Christ.

1 JOHN 1:3 NASB

Here I am! I stand at the door
and knock. If you hear my voice and
open the door, I will come in and eat
with you, and you will eat with me.

REVELATION 3:20 NCV

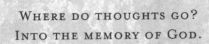

WHERE DO THOUGHTS GO?
INTO THE MEMORY OF GOD.

Reminder

Dennis was at the gas station when the alarm went off on his watch. He smiled, paused for a moment, then hit the reset button. An hour from now he'd do the same thing all over again. If people knew what he was doing, they might think he was a little over the edge. But Dennis didn't care. All he knew was that it worked.

It started as just a crazy idea, a whim. A friend mentioned how easy it was to forget God. He'd told Dennis that he bet there wasn't anyone who could remember God was right there every hour of the day. So Dennis started setting his watch. Now, every hour he was reminded of God's continual presence in his life. He knew that not a moment went by without God thinking about him. And now, he was learning to keep his thoughts on God.

God is thinking of you—right now! Think about that.

The only accurate way to understand ourselves
is by what God is and by what he does for us,
not by what we are and what we do for him.

ROMANS 12:3 THE MESSAGE

❧

As the Father hath loved me, so have
I loved you: continue ye in my love.

JOHN 15:9 KJV

❧

"Let me give you a new command: Love one
another. In the same way I loved you, you
love one another. This is how everyone will
recognize that you are my disciples—when
they see the love you have for each other."

JOHN 13:34-35 THE MESSAGE

❧

The Source of Love

Kara was just trying to be sensitive. She was always kind and tried not to let anyone down. She figured out what rubbed people the wrong way and then did the exact opposite. Being likable wasn't a bad thing, she reasoned. After all, she did everything in the name of love.

Kara finally over-committed herself into a corner one day because she thought that saying no would have been impolite. As a result, good old reliable Kara ended up letting others down. They forgave her, but forgiving herself was another matter. That day, God showed her that the person she was really trying to love was herself. It was a painful revelation, but it changed the way she related to God, others, and herself. She finally understood what real love was all about.

What makes you "valuable?" Is it what you do? What you have? Who you know? No, you are valuable because God created you, knows you intimately, and loves you completely.

> OUR ACCEPTANCE BEFORE GOD IS COMPLETE AND SECURE EVEN WHEN WE ARE DISAPPOINTED IN OURSELVES.

You are a forgiving God, gracious
and compassionate, slow to anger
and abounding in love.

NEHEMIAH 9:17

❧

My son, keep your father's commands, and
don't forget your mother's teaching. They will
guide you when you walk. They will guard you
when you sleep. They will speak to you when
you are awake. These commands are like a lamp;
this teaching is like a light. And the correction
that comes from them will help you have life.

PROVERBS 6:20, 22-23 NCV

❧

I will lead my blind people by roads they have
never traveled. I will turn their darkness into
light and make rough country smooth
before them. These are my promises,
and I will keep them without fail.

ISAIAH 42:16 TEV

❧

Deserved Rewards

The quarter fell smoothly through the coin slot. Continuing his after-school work tradition, Aaron pushed the button above his favorite candy bar. But something went awry. Out dropped a piece of fruit. Aaron uttered a few choice words. He'd been duped. He returned to the stockroom, muttering, and tossed the banana in the trash.

An hour later, he was still upset. Realizing this seemed more than a bit excessive, he asked God for some insight. What he got in return was more than he expected. Earlier that morning Aaron had asked God to help him get the promotion he'd been waiting for. It was given to another coworker instead, and Aaron had felt let down.

Many of us, consciously or unconsciously, see God as a cosmic vending machine—prayers in, and we'll get what we've "ordered." God does want the very best for us, but "God's best" isn't always what we see as best for us. It's through constantly seeking Him (not some magic formula) that we will find His desires for us.

WE LITTLE KNOW THE THINGS FOR WHICH WE PRAY.

Declare the praises of him who called you
out of darkness into his wonderful light.

1 PETER 2:9

Even the hotheads among them will be full
of sense and understanding. Those who
stammer in uncertainty will speak out plainly.

ISAIAH 32:4 NLT

The mouth of the just bringeth
forth wisdom. . . . The lips of the
righteous know what is acceptable.

PROVERBS 10:31-32 KJV

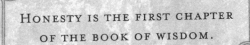

HONESTY IS THE FIRST CHAPTER
OF THE BOOK OF WISDOM.

Exposed

Larry was in the darkroom, and he was desperate. These pictures had to turn out. He had bragged about his photographic expertise to a friend. In turn, the friend asked him to take some family portraits. Larry was too embarrassed to explain that his experience with flash photography was shaky, to say the least. Instead, he just smiled, accepted his friend's money, and tried to look like he knew what he was doing.

But it looked like the prayers weren't working because the photos were too dark—every single frame. Anger, mixed with humiliation left Larry feeling exposed as a fraud in front of his friend and God. It wasn't that he was a poor photographer; he just needed more practice. And it wasn't that Larry was a bad Christian; he just needed to turn to God more often out of love, rather than desperation.

When we attempt to fool ourselves, others, or God, we never achieve the finest quality—in photography or life.

Do nothing out of selfish ambition or vain conceit, but in humility consider others better than yourselves.

PHILIPPIANS 2:3

It was for my own good that I had such troubles. Because you love me very much, you did not let me die but threw my sins far away.

ISAIAH 38:17 NCV

Strive for peace with all men, and for the holiness without which no one will see the Lord. See to it that no one fail to obtain the grace of God; that no "root of bitterness" spring up and cause trouble, and by it the many become defiled.

HEBREWS 12:14-15 RSV

Second String

When it came to playing the trumpet, Tim was without equal—at least at Central High School. But all of that changed the day Roger showed up at band rehearsal. He had just moved into town and was looking for a place where he could get "plugged in." Four bars into the first piece, Tim knew he hadn't met his match, but rather his superior.

Tim went home ready to quit the band. He decided that they didn't need him and felt like he'd been replaced. He wondered if he should give up band and try out for basketball. Despondently, he prayed for direction.

What do you think Tim heard in response to his prayers? Have you ever been in a position to hear a similar response? Think about what you are good at. Do you often compare yourself with others in this area? Take a few moments to talk to God about the talents and abilities present in your life. Then, remember always to look to God for approval, not other people. He is committed to drawing out the very best in every person.

COMPARISON, MORE THAN REALITY, MAKES MEN HAPPY OR WRETCHED.

Acknowledgements

Francis Quarles (7); Hannah Hurnard (9); Mary Bryant (21); Oliver Wendell Holmes (23); Bertha Munroe (29); Thomas Lamance (33); William Arthur Ward (45); Erwin W. Lutzer (47, 199); Cardinal John Henry Newman (51); R. C. Sproul (53); Alfred North Whitehead (55); John Chrysostom (59); Phillip James Bailey (61); Charles Haddon Spurgeon (63); George MacDonald (65), A. W. Tozer (67, 177, 187); Agnes Maude Royden (69); Leigh Nygard (73), The Berdiche Rabbi (75); Billy Zeoli (77); Eugene Gladstone O'Neill (79); Oswald Chambers (81), Algernon Charles Swinburne (89); Robert Cecil (91); Ralph Waldo Emerson (95); Meister Eckhart (109); Robert Louis Stevenson (123); Søren Kierkegaard (127); Benjamin Franklin (133, 143); Epicurus (147); Proverb (153); Isan McLaren (155); Robert Browning (157), William Cowper (159), Cicero (161); Anthony of Egypt (165); Henrik Ibsen (167); from *The Cloud of Unknowing* (169); Jean Paul Sartre (171); Publilius Syrus (173, 195); George Washington (175); Winston Churchill (179); Adam Clarke (181); William Shakespeare (183); Izzak Walton (185); F.B. Meyer (189); John Chrysostom (191); Mechthild of Magdeburg (193); Joseph Joubert (197); Geoffrey Chaucer (201); Thomas Jefferson (203), Thomas Fuller (205).

Additional copies of this book and other titles from
Honor Books are available from your local bookstore.

Also Available:

E-mail from God for Teens
God's Little Devotional Book for Teens
God's Little Lessons for Teens
God Speaks Stories for Teens
In the Chat Room with God
More E-mail from God for Teens
My Personal Promise Bible for Teens
Real Teens, Real Stories, Real Life

If you have enjoyed this book,
or if it has impacted your life,
we would like to hear from you.

Please contact us at:

Honor Books
Department E
P.O. Box 55388
Tulsa, Oklahoma 74155
Or by e-mail at *info@honorbooks.com*